SO-AHX-734

DATE DUE

PRINTED IN U.S.A.

Black Death White Hands

PAUL R. WILSON

Black Death
White Hands

GEORGE ALLEN & UNWIN
Sydney   London   Boston

© Paul R. Wilson 1982
This book is copyright under the Berne Convention.
No reproduction without permission. All rights
reserved.

First published in 1982 by
George Allen & Unwin Australia Pty Ltd
8 Napier Street, North Sydney, NSW 2060 Australia

George Allen & Unwin (Publishers) Ltd
Park Lane, Hemel Hempstead, Herts HP2 4TE
England

Allen & Unwin Inc
9 Winchester Terrace, Winchester, Mass 01890 USA

National Library of Australia
Cataloguing-in-Publication entry:

Wilson, Paul R. (Paul Richard), 1941—.
Black death, white hands.

Includes index.

ISBN 0 86861 300 2
ISBN 0 86861 308 8 (pbk.)

[1]. Aborigines, Australian–Crime–Social
aspects. [2]. Aborigines, Australian–Crime–
Economic aspects. [3]. Aborigines, Australian–
Crime–Political aspects. I. Title.

364.3'49915

Library of Congress Catalog Card Number:
82–71289

Set in 10 on 11 pt Century by Setrite Typesetters
Printed in Hong Kong by Wing King Tong Co., Ltd.

Contents

Introduction *vii*

1 **Black death** *1*
The death of Deidre — More death — White hands

2 **Killing my brother** *10*
Who, how and why? — A pattern repeated — People who kill

3 **Self-mutilation, the alternative** *22*
Another form of violence — A common occurrence — Old customs

4 **Death of the Dreamtime** *35*
Life before whites — The process of destruction — Aboriginality: what is left?

5 **White man's drugs** *48*
Violence and alcohol — A culture of drinking — Multiple causes, multiple solutions

6 **Killing me quietly** *64*
The spectre of imprisonment — The other side of death — The consequences

7 **The official weapons** *79*
On powerlessness and prejudice — The political weapons — The economic and social weapons

8 **Ending the slaughter** *96*
A country's stigma — New directions

9 **A choice of futures** *111*
A chain of violence — The past repeated — A man called Alwyn Peter

Notes *120*

Index *146*

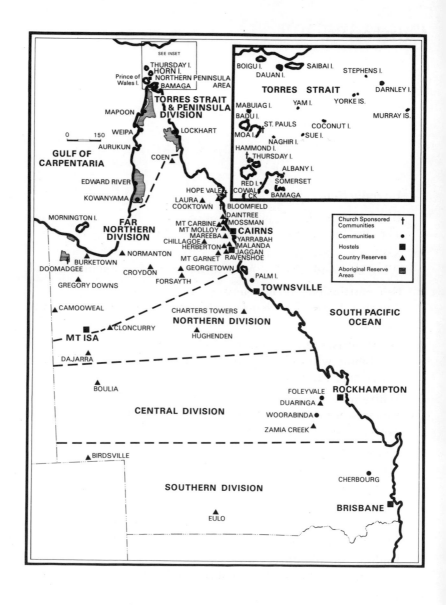

Introduction

This book originated during research I conducted for the trial of Alwyn Peter, a young Aboriginal man from Weipa South charged with killing his girlfriend. The Public Defender, Bill O'Connor, decided to make the Alwyn Peter trial a test case. The question was whether Alwyn's actions could be explained, if not justified, by historical events surrounding his life.

O'Connor assigned one of his solicitors, Peter Clapin, to prepare instructions for the barrister defending Alwyn. It was decided that Des Sturgess, undoubtedly the best known and most experienced criminal barrister in Queensland, would be offered Alwyn's defence. Sturgess accepted the brief and worked closely with Peter Clapin during the research leading up to the trial.

Peter Clapin's task was enormous. He had to thoroughly investigate all facets of Alwyn's life, and reconstruct a history of a people — Alwyn's descendants, the Mapoon people — from scattered and fragmentary sources. His ability to do this was one of the outstanding features of the case, and his written account of Alwyn's life and the Mapoon people's history served all of us who were involved in the trial with invaluable background information.

With Clapin's permission I have drawn heavily from his notes and records when discussing certain features of Alwyn's life. Clapin went well beyond what was expected of him during the months preceeding the trial. He worked closely with the junior counsel for the trial, Frank Brennan, a young criminal lawyer with a highly developed social conscience and respect for the Aboriginal people. Brennan's sincerity and humanity impressed all of us who worked on the case. Alwyn, the Aboriginal people of Queensland and those who strive to understand the black experience owe him much.

The Public Defender elicited a great deal of expert evidence during the course of the trial. Psychologists, psychiatrists, anthropologists and doctors contributed stimulating and relevant reports, many of which are referred to and acknowledged in this book. Particular thanks are due to John Taylor, an anthropologist from James Cook University, Townsville, and two young and perceptive anthropologists from the University of Queensland, David Trigger and Chris Anderson. David and Chris were especially helpful in discussing with me the complexities of the diverse Aboriginal communities in Queensland and in attuning me to relevant scholarship and research on Aboriginal matters.

Des Sturgess, an intelligent and insightful barrister, displayed a crusading zeal combined with a legal acuteness that was absolutely essential in such a trial. Sturgess epitomised the best of the legal tradition — humanity combined with conscientious advocacy for his client.

The other person who commanded the respect of everyone associated with the Alwyn Peter case was my research assistant, Robyn Lincoln. When Clapin and Sturgess asked me to investigate the amount of serious crime occurring on Aboriginal reserves, the task appeared almost impossible. We were running short of time, data was lacking, and the co-operation of Queensland Government Departments was problematical to say the least. Robyn coped with all these problems with a cheerful and calm disposition that inspired us all. After the trial, Ms Lincoln displayed the same characteristics when preparing background material for this book. Her sensitivity to the issues involved in Aboriginal violence, and her empathy with Aboriginal people, helped me considerably in writing this book. I owe her much and I hope this manuscript does justice to her efforts.

Others who assisted me during research for the trial and the book include Dr Mukherjee from the Australian Institute of Criminology, Matt Foley from the University of Queensland's Social Work Department and Professor Don McElwain from the University of Queensland's Psychology Department. Mention should also be made of the insights of *Courier-Mail* feature writer, Don Petersen, whose articles on the case inspired me to investigate fully the historical and social antecedents of Alwyn's case. Social worker Anne McKinnon provided invaluable information in her reports for the Alwyn Peter case and other trials. These enabled me to gain an understanding of the background factors associated with violent offenders and offences.

Sylvia Monk was good enough to provide me with the transcripts of her conversations with Aboriginal people on reserves during her tour of Queensland in 1981. Pat Noonan from Mackay read earlier drafts of this work and gave me some valuable insights into Aboriginal alcoholism. My publisher, John Iremonger, offered me more than most other publishers have. Jenny, my typist from the University of Queensland, gave me remarkably clear and quick first drafts for which I am extremely grateful.

All the cases in this book occurred exactly as stated. I have used first names only in order to provide some anonymity for individuals and their families, except for the Peter family. I have avoided using numbers in the text to refer to notes, but instead have included an extensive resource and note section at the end of the book.

Four black men and women whom I have known during the course of my life allowed me to understand Aboriginality to an extent that would not otherwise have been possible. Michael Mace gave me insight into reasons underlying the anger that many Aborigines feel, and Rose Colless, my friend from Douglas House in Cairns, showed me the compassion and wisdom that many of her race display. My personal friendship with Bobbi Sykes over a number of years allowed me to learn just how deeply political oppression affects personal behaviour and thought. Finally, Alwyn Peter was the person whose history fuelled me to write this book.

In writing this account of violence and death, I realised that the book would not bring credit to Queensland or Australia. The stories that unfold in the following pages are full of pathos and despair. They reflect badly on our State and federal political leaders and indeed on the basic humanity of Australians. But the story had to be told, if only because we still have the chance to redeem ourselves as a nation. Possessed by a development ideology, we often conveniently forget the suffering and humiliation that our economic 'progress' has inflicted on Aboriginal and Islander people. If we as a nation are to balance the books, to show that we have a human as well as a materialistic face, we will have to deal honestly with the causes of black violence no matter how painful this may be. Only when we have done this, can we propose realistic and constructive policies designed to stop black men and women from killing each other.

1 Black Death

The Death of Deidre

On 8 September 1981, Alwyn Peter, a young Aboriginal man from Weipa South, appeared in court charged with manslaughter. On the same day, local and State politicians were proudly predicting the success of the 1982 Commonwealth Games. The politicians were quick to point out that the world's Press would promote Queensland's boom.

There would be much for the television cameras to capture: the high-rise buildings and freeways of the once sleepy city of Brisbane; the corpulent affluence of the Gold Coast; the flourishing holiday resorts along the Barrier Reef. Queenslanders are proud of their young but prosperous State, for out of desert and coastline they have created a region rich in cattle-grazing, mining and industrial development.

However, not all Queenslanders have shared in the prosperity of their State. Alwyn Peter did not have a prosperous background. He and his family belong to a race whose cultural heritage goes back 40,000 years, but their land was taken away under lease to a mining company. They were evicted from their homes, which were later burnt down by white men. The Peters were then forced to live on government reserves, under conditions which most white Queenslanders would find intolerable.

Murder, self-mutilation and alcoholism are rife in these communities. People of differing tribes and from various areas mix with each other in an atmosphere of tension and violence. Traditional food gathering practices of hunting and fishing are limited, and the language and rituals of their forefathers have been almost forgotten.

These facts probably seemed irrelevant to Alwyn as he stood before Mr Justice Dunn to answer a charge of manslaughter. Alwyn, 24, had killed his girlfriend, Deidre, 19, by stabbing her to death. Standing in the dock, surrounded by a sea of white faces, Alwyn must have been confused by the words read out to His Honour by the Crown Prosecutor, Tom Wakefield:

> The accused is an Aboriginal who has lived only on missions. He and the deceased, who were living together, had returned to the mission at Weipa only shortly before the incident which led to the death. Shortly before 9.30 p.m. on 7 December (1979), the accused stabbed the deceased once in the back with a fairly long sharp knife. The blade penetrated through the lung, the pericardal sac and the heart. A post-mortem examination established that death was due to haemopericardium resulting from a penetrating chest wound. Penetration distance was from 9 to 10 centimetres. The wound was inflicted in a bedroom in a house which the accused and deceased had been occupying since their return to the mission.

These events were not recalled clearly by Alwyn. It transpired during the hearing that he had been very drunk at the time of the killing. He told police that he had only meant half the blade to penetrate as he did not want to seriously injure Deidre: he had wanted to 'stick her but not kill her'. He could not, he said in court, remember saying many of the things to police that he was alleged to have said. All he really knew was that he gave police an incorrect version of how the stabbing occurred because he had loved Deidre so much, he did not give a damn what happened to him.

Not 'giving a damn' what happened to him has been a characteristic life strategy adopted by Alwyn. During the court hearings, evidence was presented which described his existence as aimless and destructive. Plagued by illness, and caught between the old ways of his parents and grandparents, and the new ways of Weipa South, Alwyn drifted from job to prison to unemployment. His adolescence was punctuated by fights, many of which originated while he was on 'hot stuff', the local term for wine and spirits. He had inherited a world of deprivation, friction and frequent violence.

In pleading Alwyn Peter's case before Mr Justice Dunn, Des Sturgess explained Alwyn's plight in his opening remarks:

> Our case is shortly this: In Queensland, there have been created communities in which the incidence of homicide and very serious assaults is amongst the highest that has been reached and published anywhere in the world. It is, for example,

thought to be at least equivalent to that which is found in the poorest and the most violent ghettos of New York. Now, Deidre Gilbert, the deceased girl, and Alwyn Peter, the prisoner, were members of one such community, and they were shaped by it and each has been destroyed by it. Now, I should tell your Honour that to be a member of such a community one does not have to be mad or bad, but one only has to be an Aborigine . . . The sad fact will emerge from all this that this young man in the dock, your Honour, has no hope and is without hope.

The real tragedy, however, is not Alwyn Peter alone. It lies with the thousands of other Aborigines who, as with Alwyn, are without hope. Deidre died at the hands of a man she loved deeply, who loved her. On Aboriginal communities in Queensland, hundreds of others share their plight.

More Death

In Queensland, as in most other States, the true picture of violence in Aboriginal communities can never really be shown. The few available studies are sketchy, to say the least, and rely on anecdote and observation rather than on empirical evidence.

The Alwyn Peter case, however, provided an opportunity to assess the extent of violent crime on Queensland Aboriginal reserves and communities. As part of the case presented in the sentence hearing, the Public Defender was able to collect dossiers and records of interviews of previous cases of violence known to the Aboriginal and Torres Strait Islander Legal Services (ATSILS) between late 1978 and July 1981.

To obtain these records, the Public Defender relied on the assistance of the ATSILS in major areas of Queensland. However, for a variety of reasons, the records of crime finally obtained were a gross under-estimation of the true number of violent offences occurring on Aboriginal communities throughout the State.

Many of the ATSILS offices paid scant attention to their record-keeping, and consequently their files were inaccurate and incomplete. Some agencies co-operated; others did not. Perhaps most importantly, many cases of violence were not reported to the police and not proceeded with in court. Violence, as we will see, is so heavily ingrained within these communities that its existence is accepted, however reluctantly, as a fact of life not requiring police attention.

Nevertheless, although the cases documented were only an

indication of the true state of violence, 82 detailed accounts were collected of charges of murder, manslaughter, grievous bodily harm, unlawful wounding and assault occasioning bodily harm that occurred on 17 Aboriginal reserves and communities throughout Queensland during the three-year period studied.

When this information was analysed, the prevalence of death and violence was astonishing. Alwyn Peter was far from unique. His pattern was often repeated, with the dossiers and transcripts revealing numerous cases of murder, manslaughter and serious assault on Queensland's Aboriginal reserves and communities. Although raw statistical figures often hide the personal agony of victims and offenders, the figures obtained were clear in their message.

Let us look first at homicide, which we defined as the combined number of murder and manslaughter charges averaged over the three-year period. We found that the homicide rate per year across the 17 communities studied was 39.6 per 100,000, compared with an annual rate for the State of Queensland of 3.28 per 100,000, and a national rate of 4.00 per 100,000. Thus the homicide rate for Aborigines living on Queensland reserves is 10 times the national and State average. When it is remembered that these figures are a gross under-estimation of the true state of violence, their implications are startlingly clear: black men and women are killing each other at a rate which far exceeds their counterparts in other sectors of the State and nation.

Nowhere was this trend made clearer than by a comparison of the homicide rate in Aboriginal communities with other centres in Queensland. For example, the Southern Queensland region, comprising the towns of Charleville, Toowoomba, Dalby, Roma and Warwick, has a total population of 201,000 people and a homicide rate of 0.99 per 100,000. The North Brisbane region, comprising the inner-city Brisbane area and the city of Redcliffe, has a total population of 478,000 and a rate of 1.67; the figure for Mt Isa and Townsville, cities with a combined population of 184,000, was 4.99 per 100,000. Thus the rate for homicide on the Aboriginal reserves and communities studied is 8–40 times greater than for other regional centres in the State.

Comparisons can be made with overseas countries. For example, the rates for homicide in the United Kingdom are 1.4 per 100,000; in Canada 5.7; in Western Germany 4.1; in the United States 9.0. Even within violence-ridden America, our rate of 39.6 for Aborigines is far higher than for American crime capitals. In California, a State with similar geographical and demographical features to those of Queensland, the cities of San

Francisco, Los Angeles and San Diego have homicide rates of 17.5, 24.7 and 7.82 respectively. Some figures suggest that American blacks and Indians, both crime-prone groups, have a lesser rate than Aboriginal Australians.

There is one other set of figures to be discussed before the statistical profile can be completed. These relate to the rate of serious assault — an even more conservative estimate of the true state of violence in Aboriginal communities than that of the homicide figures. Assault is far more likely than murder to be ignored by white police, to go unreported, or to be dealt with 'informally' by Aboriginal police on reserves. But even with assault we find the same bleak picture emerging from the statistics. The rate for serious assault charges on reserves is 226.05 per 100,000 compared with a Queensland figure of 43.85. So, although the reported Aboriginal rate is five times greater than for that the State as a whole, the enormous 'hidden' assault rate — crimes not reported — probably 10 to 15 times the State or national figure.

These figures mean that violence and death is such a common occurrence in black communities that every family, directly or indirectly, suffers the consequences of murder or serious assault. Often multiple tragedy affects the same family, with a violent death occurring more than once in a generation. Alwyn Peter's family exemplifies this pattern. Alwyn's brother Sidney, stabbed a girl, Geraldine, with whom he was living. Geraldine, although seriously wounded, survived, and Sidney was sentenced to jail for committing grievous bodily harm.

Geraldine then began a relationship with another man, who had previously killed his wife. This man later killed Geraldine by stabbing her with a knife. The subsequent police investigation revealed an earlier death in the family. Geraldine had previously given evidence to the murder by her father of one of his two wives.

Another case from Weipa South illustrates the typical violence found on Aboriginal communities. Oscar was accused of killing his wife Ivy, and was convicted of manslaughter. Oscar and Ivy had been married for five years and had a three-year-old child. Oscar described his marriage as 'happy' but admitted that he drank heavily and, in common with many other reserve dwellers, often beat his wife.

I didn't lose my temper often. Ivy used to lose her temper — just when I'm drunk. I have hit her before. She would hit back. I would slap her across the face and hit her with a strap across the behind. I hit her with a thick belt that I used to wear. I never hit her with a fist before. She had a cut under the eye once. She has had cut lips from where I've slapped her. When I hit her, I hit her pretty hard.

Oscar and Ivy walked along a precipice, with 'a bit of a belting' on one side and death on the other. What started off as just 'a belting' often escalated into a furious explosion of punches and kicks leading to tragedy. Oscar's account of the killing illustrates how the process of attack and counter-attack grew murderous.

It was the first time I took her to the canteen at the mission. We got there at 6.00 and left at 9.30. I was very drunk. She was not very drunk. She started to go crook at me for drinking. I told her to shut up and be quiet. I didn't like her complaining about my drinking.
     When we got to the back of the house, I lost my temper and pushed her down. I grabbed her by the back of the neck and pushed her down. She landed on her knees and her hands and she fell on her face, because I pushed her hard. I picked her up. She was still growling and trying to punch me.
     I grabbed a stick off the shelf. I hit her about the head. She was screaming, and swearing and abusing me. She was saying she would put a knife through me and saying she was going to leave me. She makes me wild and I go off my head when she says it.
     I pulled her up by the hair and pushed her forward in towards the wall. She kept hitting her head against the wall. I punched her in the face and told her to shut up. I hit her in the ribs and it was a hard one.

Oscar then went to sleep till 8 o'clock the next morning. He moved into the kitchen, ignoring the body of Ivy slumped on the floor, and made himself a cup of tea. After drinking it, he visited Ivy's mother and sat there yarning with the boys, then went down to the pub. Returning to his mother-in-law's at about a quarter to one, he was met by a police sergeant who informed him of Ivy's death.
     The sergeant took Oscar to the morgue to identify the body, interrogated him and arranged to take him back to the reserve to the scene of the attack. Oscar was reluctant to go. 'Sergeant', he said, 'I can't go back to the reserve because they kill me down there. Can I sleep here?'. The sergeant asked Oscar, 'Are you frightened to go back?', and Oscar replied, 'Yes, sergeant.
     So he should have been. Oscar, as with many other violent

offenders, knew that the friends and relatives of the victim could seek revenge that would continue the cycle of butchery. But the origins of this chain of destruction lie not with Oscar, nor with Alwyn Peter of Weipa South, but with a colonial past that few of the offenders or their victims would remember.

White Hands

When Alwyn and Oscar killed, they displayed a direct and easily recognised form of violence. There are other forms of violence, however, which do not have physical force, intentionality and criminal action as their components.

This book discusses these other, more subtle forms of violence as well as direct aggression by one Aborigine against another. Indeed, a central thesis of the research discussed in these pages is that white Australians have created historical and social conditions which are violence-provoking.

White violence against Aborigines has been extensively documented. In Tasmania, the first settlers moved across the island and exterminated all but a handful of Tasmanian Aborigines. In Queensland, an unknown observer in the young colony wrote in 1863 that Aborigines were 'shot down like wild dogs — and with as little remorse. Even poison has been used lately.'

Although not recognised as a war, along the moving Queensland frontier pastoralists battled with Aborigines over land, at first in the Moreton Bay area. As the superior firepower of the whites overwhelmed the Aborigines, atrocities mounted. The once proud warrior tribe, the Kalkadoons, fought bravely to maintain their ancestral land but by the 1890s the tribe was totally and irrevocably dispossessed. In 1878, it was estimated that the tribe consisted of 2 000 men and at least as many of women and children. Twenty-one years later, a police sergeant reported that he could only locate 101 people from the tribe. For once statistics speak more eloquently than words.

To justify the extermination and exploitation of the natives, Queensland colonists de-humanised Aborigines by comparing European with indigenous culture. Expropriation of land was rationalised by arguing that Aborigines had no government, law or society and therefore had no title to land. Stories of Aboriginal violence, cannibalism and sexual depravity enabled white settlers to justify shooting men and women for sport, much as they shot kangaroos in north Queensland.

A correspondent in the *Moreton Bay Courier* in 1858 referred to the 'wretched characteristics of our black civilization — their fearful superstition, their bestial tastes, their undisguised squalor and filth, their indolence and their nomadic disposition'. Another writer of the same period in *The Queenslander* said the Aborigines were 'one of the poorest, most barbarous, sunken and degraded races of the whole globe, with their idle, lazy and wandering mode of existence'.

These attitudes contributed markedly to the rapid decline of an indigenous race. A well based estimate puts the Aboriginal population in 1788 at about 315,000, more than one-third living in Queensland. By 1930, extermination, disease and dispersement had reduced both the Queensland and Australian Aboriginal populations to about 21,000 and 63,000 respectively.

Despite the fierce defence of their homeland by the Kalkadoons and other Queensland tribes, the colonists defined their punitive expeditions as dispersals or reprisals, rather than as military action against a well organised guerrilla force. In contrast to the history of the American Indians or the New Zealand Maoris, no Aboriginal war was recognised. As a result, no treaties were made with the tribes and no rights were established to benefit them.

Instead, dispossessed Aborigines huddled around frontier towns and were left to the whims of white economic forces. In Mackay, for example, residents initiated a scheme to settle Aborigines on reserves to obtain cheap labour for sugar plantations. In the second half of the 19th century, miners and cattle breeders, as well as the Queensland Government, rounded up and settled Aborigines on confined reserves. This process of dispossession continued right up to the mid-1960s, when the people of Mapoon in the Cape York Peninsula were forced off their traditional homelands.

The results of this European exploitation of Aborigines and Aboriginal land can be seen today. Aborigines in Queensland have been forced to live in government run or mission-controlled settlements, in communities fringing small towns, or within the poorest areas of large cities. There are for example, 14 Aboriginal and Islander reserves (now euphemistically called 'communities'), under the control of the Churches or the Queensland Department of Aboriginal and Islander Advancement, containing about one-quarter of the State's total Aboriginal population.

Other communities (the Queensland Government recognises 56; the Federal Government says 200), huddle around towns such as Mt Isa and Townsville, and many Aborigines live in what the sociologists call 'low socio-economic' areas in Brisbane. In all,

40,000 Aborigines live in Queensland, and although their population growth-rate is twice that of whites, their numbers are still
only a third of what they were before white settlers arrived.

Reserve, community and urban Aborigines have much in
common. Aborigines do not own their own land; in the city and
the country, traditional rituals, language and cultural patterns
have almost disappeared. Aboriginal reserves and communities
are scattered over vast areas of Queensland, often away from
territory to which the residents feel communal or historical ties.
Furthermore, these reserve dwellers — the victims of much of the
violence described in this book — are subjected to a series of acts
and by-laws, originating from and administered by whites, which
effectively disallow them from running their communities.

These historical forces and present social conditions have led to
what Aboriginal writer Kevin Gilbert calls 'the human desolation
of Aboriginal society'. This desolation exists not just in health,
housing, education and employment, but, more importantly, in
'what Aboriginal people have come to believe about themselves'.

In creating this desolation and powerlessness, white society
has engaged in the indirect form of aggression outlined above.
We have taken from native Australians not only their land and
their traditional ways of relating to each other and to that land,
but also their self-esteem and identity.

This desolation is, fortunately, not complete. In cities,
communities, and on reserves, distinctive Aboriginal ways of
acting and conceptualising the world still exist. Aboriginality
exists not simply in language and dance, but flows quietly in the
minds and dreams of those who live in the city and the outback
reserve. For it to be rekindled, Aborigines must have a future
that they can control, rather than a present full of malice, tension
and insecurity, determined by others.

So we return to violence. For although the violence studied is
black people killing each other, we should never forget the
historical and social roots of that violence. Whites have, by
political, legal and sometimes police action, created conditions
which foster murder and assault in Aboriginal communities. A
central thesis of this book is that we cannot divorce the sense of
hopelessness and futility that exists among Aborigines — born of
dispossession and exploitation — from Alwyn's knife or Oscar's
raised fist. The network of violence in Aboriginal communities,
which we look at in chapter 2, will remain invisible to us to the
extent that we ourselves obscure our own violent past
and present.

2 Killing My Brother

Who, How and Why?

Murder in most societies typically occurs among relatives and friends, and is heavily concentrated within working-class families. Indeed, observers of violence have often pointed out that the family is the greatest repository of violence outside maximum-security prisons. North Queensland reserve Aborigines exemplify this pattern. Only two of the 82 cases of violence we studied involved an offence where a stranger or an outsider was the victim.

Aboriginal offenders parallel violent offenders in general, who are usually working-class males. Obviously, reserve dwellers are from the lower socio-economic stratum of Australian society and most offenders in our study were male. Women were particularly vulnerable to violence, especially if they were living with men. Indeed, in 55 per cent of cases, the relationship of the attacker to the victim was marital or de facto, as with Alwyn killing Deidre or Oscar murdering Ivy. In contrast to white society, in which middle-class domestic violence is quite common but not often reported, Aboriginal communities emulate their working-class white counterparts by publically displaying violence.

Nothing could illustrate more clearly the breakdown of traditional society than the violence inflicted by men on their women. As we will see, jealousy was often the immediate motive behind stabbing or punching, although other motives were present too. In traditional society, specific punishments including death were inflicted by those aggrieved on unfaithful women, but these punishments were socially sanctioned and approved by the tribe. However, in traditional society, men would offer their women to friends and enemies either as a mark of esteem or as a way of pacifying inter-tribal feuds.

Violence against women in north Queensland reserves is very different. It is not approved by the community nor confined to cases of infidelity. Often the infidelity is imagined by the offender to rationalise his general feelings of frustration and aggression.

Not all violence revealed in our study was of this kind. The dossiers revealed many cases of daughter killing father, brother killing brother, and brother killing sister. Numerous cases recorded brothers fighting among themselves. One, for example, grabbed a kitchen knife and stabbed another. In many other cases, sons and daughters used knives or forks to stab their fathers or mothers.

Most murders and assaults, however, were what is commonly known in the criminological literature as 'marital murder'. A typical example was Percy, who killed his wife Annie at Edward River Mission. Percy had married Annie when he was 30, after living with her for some years. No one knew Annie's exact age, although Percy thought Annie had been very young, about 12, when he met her. They had a church wedding, because Percy had wanted it that way — Christianity was very important to him. Percy had said he loved Annie very much, and over seven years she bore him five children.

According to the social worker who interviewed him, Percy was 'a quiet, co-operative, mature Aboriginal man of average intelligence, limited articulation and a low degree of acculturation into white society'. Percy had worked at various jobs on the reserve after leaving school — labouring, herding cattle, cleaning, and later he became a member of the Edward River police force.

This 'quiet, co-operative, mature Aboriginal man', however, as with many others, was capable of killing the person he loved most. At about 5.00 p.m. on 30 November 1978, Percy and Annie went to the Edward River canteen, bought some cans of beer and sat down with some friends on the grass around the canteen.

Annie and Percy quarrelled and Annie ran away and joined another group of men and women drinking. Percy followed and forced her to come home with him, later admitting that both of them had been very drunk. According to Percy, he asked his wife why she ran away and Annie responded by saying 'that's my business'. Percy then got up and hit his wife with the hunting stick he kept in the bedroom.

Percy thought he hit Annie three or four times on the back and three times on the head. Annie sat down in the bedroom doorway, screamed loudly and held her head between her legs. Percy could not remember whether he hit her again but he could remember saying to Annie, 'let's go to bed now', and they had both lain on the mattress.

Percy went straight to sleep. On waking up the next morning

he did not find Annie next to him and hurried around the house looking for her. He found her lying dead on the floor of the front room. Percy broke down and cried before getting the neighbours.

According to the social worker's report, Percy loved and cared for his wife. The report stated that Percy appeared greatly distressed and distraught to think that he had lost his wife through an act he had not intended. According to the social worker, Percy frequently cried at night when thinking of the incident. Percy, in a statement to the police, confirmed the social worker's observations by saying, 'I didn't mean to hurt her badly, I just wanted to hit her slightly, but I didn't know what I was doing'.

Percy's cry was echoed by other Aboriginal killers. A thorough analysis of the homicides on the reserves gave some credence to this cry. In only four cases was there some forethought of violence; all the other cases displayed elements of spontaneous attacks, erupting as the result of a perceived provocation or a drunken brawl, which quickly ran out of control. Other men who had killed their wives or de factos said that they 'just wanted to teach her a lesson' or 'to hurt her a bit' but never to kill.

Of course, it is easy for anyone who kills or maims to rationalise their motives afterwards, by saying that they did not mean to do it. But by looking at the degree of force used, the type of weapon and the behaviour of the attacker after the incident, it is possible to gain a better understanding of such violent incidents.

In 30 per cent of cases, feet and hands were the methods of attack; in 42 per cent of assaults, a knife was used. Often the knife was for domestic purposes and was grabbed spontaneously to strike the victim.

Most of the attacks led to serious injury or death. Our analysis revealed that 30 per cent resulted in death; 25 per cent in permanent and severe damage; 34 per cent hospitalised the victim (the remainder could not be classified because of the lack of information). A common pattern is exemplified by a young man who came home drunk, sat down to dinner and was teased by his brother. The drunken man took his knife and fork and stabbed his brother in the arm causing fatal injuries. However, the police records showed that the younger brother had inflicted only one stab with the knife into the other's arm, but this also pierced the chest wall and resulted in death.

Despite the severity of the injuries, very little of the force involved in the violent acts could be categorised as severe. Only 12 per cent of all acts were administered with severe force, and these usually involved cases in which a knife was thrust heavily into a chest; a bottle deliberately broken and slashed deeply across a face; or a head repeatedly banged on the ground. Most of the violence was administered without much deliberate effort: for example, slapping with open hands; hitting on the nose with a beer bottle; or punching without too much force into a face or a chest.

The level of physical force involved in most homicides and assaults, as in the case above, often appeared slight in comparison with the serious results. Furthermore, confirmation of this pattern was found when the degree of premeditation in the attack was considered. In half the cases, premeditation was lacking; the offender displayed anger as a result of an insult during a drinking party. In another 10 per cent of cases, the offenders were attempting to protect someone else or themselves from violence; inadequate information in the remaining cases precluded classification of motives.

Ascertaining the cause of or motive for a crime is, as we will see, a complex and difficult process. But in the behaviour of the offender after the violence, we found definite evidence of lack of intent to kill or seriously injure. Percy, for example, hit his wife three or four times on the head and then went to bed with her and attempted to have sex, thinking that she was alive. Many of the other attackers we studied displayed the same behaviour, often picking the body of their wife or girlfriend up from the floor and taking them to the bed intending to have sexual intercourse. In the morning they would wake up horrified to find a corpse lying next to them.

The frequent lack of real intent to kill or maim is not unusual. The rate of violence on Aboriginal reserves is high, but most fights and arguments do not lead to death or serious injury. However, in some of these altercations, an extra punch or kick in a long chain of punches or kicks can be one too many. Serious injury or death occurs, much to the amazement of the perpetrator who, after years of seeing the person he or she attacks get up and carry on, is amazed to see the victim dead.

A Pattern Repeated

Despite the lack of intent to seriously injure or kill in some offenders, many reserve dwellers repeatedly committed violent acts. In 51 per cent of the cases we studied, the offenders had previous charges or convictions, and in 35 per cent of these the prior conviction was serious. This pattern is well illustrated in the death of Geraldine, the de facto wife of Alwyn's brother, Sidney Peter. Geraldine's father Harold killed his first wife, and Geraldine was killed by the man she later married, who had killed his first wife. Another man, George, was charged with unlawful and grievous bodily harm to his de facto wife after inserting a broken crutch into her vagina. When released on bail, he killed his wife by banging her head on the ground.

Harold, George, Alwyn and Sidney were conditioned to living in a climate of violence. Violence was all around them from the moment of birth. It was shared by them as offenders, and by others on the reserves and communities who might never be charged with a criminal act. Rachel Peter, mother of Alwyn, summed it up well when she said, 'at Weipa South some people fight for no reason whether they're drunk or not'. Alwyn himself recounts his childhood and adolescence in terms of fights, battles and vendettas. It was not unusual, according to Alwyn, for fights to develop between youngsters from Mapoon and the Torres Strait Islands. Knives and chains would often be used and participants were sometimes quite severely injured.

This was not the only violence Alwyn had been exposed to. He talked to his lawyer about seeing his mother and father fighting with fists and feet; about the drunken brawls that occurred at the canteen; and about his own street fighting. Very often, the Peters would discipline young Alwyn when he was bad by beating him with a belt. Alwyn, in common with many others, quickly learnt that violence was the method most people used in Weipa South to exert control and to settle disputes.

When the cases of violent crime on reserves were systematically analysed, we found that in 82 per cent of all cases of homicide and serious assault, the offenders were previously involved in severe gang fighting, drunken brawls or wife-beating. In about the same proportion, the victims of violence remembered similar instances. Offenders and victims were bound in a web of violence also by their similar home environments, which were marked by frequent physical fights between their parents. Geraldine remembered her upbringing when she gave a statement to lawyers representing her father, Harold:

> They (Harold and his wife Beryl) have always been fighting and arguing with one another when they have been drinking together. I have seen Harold hit Beryl on many occasions when they have been drunk. I have seen him punch Beryl with his closed fist while she has been laying asleep on the mattress on

the floor. I have seen him punch her all over the body, the face and the head . . . because she was too drunk to get up and cook him a meal. He has also been drunk on these occasions. I can recall that on many occasions he has picked up stones, sticks and empty wine flagons to hit Beryl with but I have managed to take them off him.

Percy, the man who killed his wife Annie at Edward River Mission, had had similar experiences. Percy told a social worker who was preparing a court report for use at his trial, of a very strict and violent upbringing, during which he was often beaten by his parents.

He also remembered his mother and father engaging in frequent arguments, usually shouting, yelling or slapping each other with their hands, although sometimes they used nulla nullas. Sometimes these fights would lead to his mother bleeding from wounds inflicted by the nulla nullas. Percy said that these fights would make him feel very sad and sorry for his mother, and very confused. As a result, he often used to run away from home, only to be brought back and severely punished by his father.

People do not often die from the clenched fist or drawn knife, so the risks attached to regular physical assault are not fully recognised. In marital disputes for example, many years of fighting between husband and wife becomes accepted by both parties with little thought given to its potential lethality. Blows are exchanged, objects are hurled, knives are thrust and in most instances, people do not die. In marital disputes or in gang fights, violence continues, indeed often escalates, after an initial exchange of blows. For, if violence is the only recourse known to people who are frustrated, who wish to resolve a dispute, the violence has to continue if the dispute is to come to any conclusion.

Violent solutions are the most common responses displayed by Aboriginal men and women to the problems and difficulties that arise in everyday life on reserves. Although not accepted by the community, homicide and assault are still seen as typical behaviours by young, old, male and female. Traditional communities had, to white eyes at least, barbaric punishments, but these were inflicted under specific conditions approved by tribal law. The people we have discussed so far — those that bash their wives, beat their children and occasionally kill their brothers, fathers or sisters — are operating in a much more diffuse and unstructured social context.

People Who Kill

This pattern of violence is diverse. The degree to which men assault their women or violate their children varies from one reserve to another, according to the extent of tribal disintegration or Europeanisation that has occurred. On many reserves, for example, children are still treated with great reverence and tolerance. They are given much warmth and affection by friends and relatives and made welcome when visiting. Up till the age of 10, physical punishment by parents is rare, although it is not uncommon for fathers to come into physical conflict with their adolescent sons, especially when drinking.

But the large number of reserve dwellers who recounted their childhood and adolescence in terms of drunken fathers who frightened them, who told of frequent physical fights between their mothers and fathers and of general community violence, strongly suggests that traditional ways of acting between children, parents, husbands and wives have long ago disappeared. Community disintegration is common on Aboriginal reserves in Queensland.

When the indices of this disintegration — homicide and assault cases — were analysed further, it was apparent that two main elements were generally present. The first was alcohol (discussed in Chapter 5). The second was jealousy or the feeling that a woman had not been faithful or was 'playing around'; this was a common factor in all the cases of men who killed their de factos or wives. Alwyn, for example, said he had killed Deidre, while drinking, because he had been jealous concerning her past relationship with another man.

The dual factors of drinking and jealousy can be seen in the case of Russell, 17, who was charged with killing his sixteen-year-old girlfriend at Mornington Island. This case was of particular interest because the court hearing occurred soon after Alwyn Peter's well-publicised trial.

On 21 February 1981, Russell had, within an hour, consumed at least ten cans of beer and by his own admission was 'very drunk'. When he left the canteen early in the evening, his girlfriend's sister told him that his girlfriend, Shirley, was up on the hill with another youth. Russell went looking for her and found Shirley engaged in sexual intercourse with the boy. Four other young men were standing by watching them. They all ran off when Russell approached.

What followed was an episode of violence very different from the apparently unintended deaths that have been discussed above. There was no gradual escalation of aggression. Instead, jealousy fuelled hate and vengeance in a fury of aggression that ended in tragedy.

Russell chased Shirley down to the river at the bottom of the hill and when she jumped in he followed her, eventually catching her by the throat. He held her head under the water until she was nearly unconscious and then dragged her from the water. Russell ripped her dress off and punched her heavily four times in the face. Shirley broke free and ran across to the other side of a nearby bridge. Russell caught her again and pushed her into the water. He held her head under and drowned her. Then he dragged her out of the water and left her naked body on the sand.

Behind Russell's case however, and other cases where jealousy and alcohol seem the obvious causes of violence, lie deeper and more complex reasons for the attacks. In some cases, such as one brother killing another, or a daughter killing her father, jealousy and alcohol are not the apparent motives.

The deeper reasons for murder and assault become more apparent after an analysis of the specific rates of violence on each reserve and community in our study. In this analysis we attempted to locate the social and cultural factors that distinguished reserves and communities from one another.

To make this distinction, two anthropologists with many years field experience on Queensland Aboriginal communities rated each reserve on a number of criteria, including such factors as the density of population, the degree of isolation from white communities, the presence of traditional culture and the availability of alcohol.

This exercise was complex. For example, in rating the degree of traditionality present, the anthropologists had to consider a number of matters, including the use of language, hunting activities, ceremonies and food-preparation skills. The degree of isolation from white contact was decided by assessing not only the number of whites present on the reserve, but also how accessible whites were by road or sea. In rating each reserve, careful note was taken of the origins of the reserve — whether they received people from other tribes or whether they were more homogenous, containing only Aborigines from the same area or group.

The results were clear-cut. We found two distinct clusters of reserves. One cluster had a very high rate of violence and the other was relatively low, although the latter rate was high by white standards. Examples of communities where violence rates

were high included Palm Island, Weipa South and Yarrabah,
where the average rate of violence was 7.07 per 1000 people.
Those in the low-violence group (with a violence rating of 2.31 per
1000) include Lockhart, Doomadgee and Aurukun.

High-violence reserves were marked by a number of characteristics: alcohol was legally available; they had only low to
medium levels of traditional culture; they had relatively high
populations; most importantly, they were reserves that had
received displaced Aborigines from other areas. Palm Island was
originally established as a penal settlement. Weipa South had
taken in people forcibly removed by police from their tribal lands
at Mapoon, as well as others from Aurukun and Edward River.
Yarrabah has people from a number of tribes.

Reserves with lower rating had nearly the reverse pattern: they
were communities in which alcohol was not legally available;
where relatively high levels of traditional culture survived; they
had low populations; they were generally isolated from white
influence; they were not receivers of people forced from their
traditional areas.

These trends in violence and destruction on Aboriginal reserves
point to explanations which are familiar to observers of other
societies. Whenever there is a lack of community cohesion,
considerable mobility from one area to another and tribal disharmony, crime and violence rates escalate.

Let us take these issues one by one. Many of the homicide
offenders were people who had been displaced from their traditional homelands and forced to live on a reserve. Alwyn Peter was
one. As discussed in greater detail later, Alwyn's parents were
taken from their traditional homeland of Mapoon and resettled in
'foreign' land at Weipa South. Alwyn, in preliminary interviews
leading up to his court appearance, felt very strongly about the
loss of tribal land; about not belonging anywhere.

Percy also came from an unstable background. His father had
two former wives, who had died, and Percy recalled that in his
childhood eight people had lived in a nine-by-ten cabbage-tree hut
at Edward River. When his mother was bashed by his father,
Percy would frequently run away. His mother died when he was
nine years old, which left him with feelings of great sadness.

When Percy was 12, his family moved to the Mitchell River
Mission, and three years later Percy went to Normanton. After a
year he returned to the Edward River Mission. Percy felt that
when the Government took over Edward River, enormous
changes occurred in his life and in the lives of other people in the

community. Wood and metal were supplied for houses; wages were paid for employment; not long after, alcohol became available in the canteen. On balance, Percy saw these changes as being highly disruptive to a community that prospered by living in more traditional ways free from the influence of alcohol and white market forces.

Mobility is also demonstrated by the number of offenders who marry or move into a de facto relationship with partners from other areas and other tribes, that have no ties with their own tribes or areas. Thus Harold, born at Weipa, married Vida from Mapoon and when she died, married Beryl from Palm Island. Such relationships between individuals of different areas were common in traditional society, but their form now lacks the rigid rules and customs on inter-tribal relationships practised by Aborigines before the white man arrived.

Individual mobility is extremely high among Aborigines, and is another critical factor contributing to the lack of community cohesion on reserves. In analysing the cases, we were struck by the number of times the offenders and their victims had either voluntarily or involuntarily moved from one area to another. For example, a typical case concerns a young man, John, born at Palm Island, who was charged with unlawful wounding.

When John was five years old, his parents moved to St Lawrence. John then spent his twelfth year back on Palm Island before moving to Ayr where he stayed for one year. He was later sentenced to spend six months at Westbrooke juvenile prison in Brisbane, before moving voluntarily to Townsville. John was then sentenced to 12 months in Stuart Creek prison. After this, John lived at Kingaroy, Mareeba, Townsville and Cairns, finally moving back to Mareeba where he committed the offence found in the dossiers.

Alwyn Peter moved frequently between Mapoon and Weipa, and was forced to go to Townsville, hundreds of miles from his home, when he was sentenced to prison. Alwyn and his mother both said they were happier on their traditional homeland at Mapoon, with familiar hunting and fishing grounds, no canteen and, equally important, with few people from different tribes and different areas.

The tribal disharmony on many reserves is a major factor blocking community cohesion. Alwyn, for example, often referred to the disharmony that resulted from people of different tribes living at Weipa South. In that small area of one square mile, this disharmony was obvious. There was, for example, 130 Torres

Strait Islanders, 111 people from Mapoon, 215 from Weipa, 9 from Aurukun and 78 from other centres. The Mapoon people were often told to go back to where they came from and fights would break out between different tribes, especially between Aborigines and Torres Strait Islanders.

The animosity between the latter two groups did not exist before the white man arrived; Aborigines and Islanders had lived in relative harmony, at a distance. However, when they were forced together into reserve areas, the Islanders found it easier to adapt to Westernised living; they obtained work, and antagonism between them and Aborigines developed.

Interlaced with all these factors are social conditions that on most reserves are appallingly bad by almost any standard. These conditions are discussed below, but the economic and community deprivation on Queensland reserves can be inferred from some salient characteristics of criminal offenders. In 53 per cent of our cases, the attacker was unemployed; in 70 per cent of instances he or she had only primary school education to Grade Seven. Most offenders existed on a weekly income of between $39 and $77 per week; only 20 per cent earned more.

Most people who killed or assaulted others lived in over-crowded houses. For example, 90 per cent of offenders lived in large family units, forced into European-style houses which were often of inferior design. At Weipa South, 62 of the 88 houses are of the older, low-set style and are desperately in need of repair. These houses, set on concrete slabs, usually have only two or three rooms, with no bathroom or laundry. In some, the tin surfaces act as heat conductors, making the inside like a furnace during summer.

The health of the person charged with a criminal offence and of their near relatives was invariably poor. In nearly 70 per cent of cases where we could obtain information, the offender was said to be in poor health, and in almost every case the offender's family had a history of severe illness and premature death. Alwyn and most of his immediate family were in poor health for most of their lives. In another case we found that the accused's parents died from opium addiction when he was young; his first and second wives died from illnesses, and three of his seven children died in early adulthood. Most of the offenders mentioned in this book had similar histories of death and illness among their immediate family.

The search for the causes of the violence that has been documented so far goes well beyond jealousy and alcohol — explanations often given by well-meaning politicians and judges. Some of those factors lie embedded in history, in the destruction of traditional Aboriginal society which occurred with the advent of the first whites. This process of Europeanisation led to the forced removal of people from one area to another, to the aimless mobility and marriage patterns found in so many Aborigines, and to the eradication of most of the traditional ways of relating to each other.

These factors, combined with poor employment health and housing conditions on white-owned and white-controlled Aboriginal communities, produce community disintegration, purposelessness and feelings of personal worthlessness. Such a condition has an inevitable result: people become violent towards others and themselves.

3 Self-mutilation

Another Form of Violence

Alwyn Peter was normally quiet and introspective, preferring to listen to others rather than initiate conversation. According to his friends and relatives, after a few beers he would change somewhat and recount jokes and anecdotes about incidents at home or work.

This quiet, friendly man was capable of changing his mood drastically. As Deidre discovered, when Alwyn drank wine or spirits, he often became a person to be feared. For when Alwyn was drunk and angry about real or supposed wrongs, one of two actions followed: he would deliberately seek a fight with a relative or friend, or he would hurt himself in some way.

When Alwyn and Deidre fought, Deidre would sometimes be hurt. But she was not the only person to suffer. When Alwyn, Sidney or both were drunk, fierce fist-fights eventuated with quite serious injuries occurring. On one occasion, Sidney struck Alwyn hard on the head with a rock, causing Alwyn to seek hospital treatment. On other occasions Alwyn fought fierce battles with his father, Simon Peter, which were often stopped only after his mother Rachel intervened.

Relatives and friends were not the sole objects of Alwyn's anger. He would often hurt or mutilate himself, especially when alcohol and small frustrations combined to compound his aggression. Alwyn's mother recalled that Alwyn would often punch and kick the glass louvres at their small house in Prunning Street, Weipa South, after her son arrived home drunk and found out there was no meat for dinner.

When Alwyn 'went mad', he would smash louvres or break furniture. Other members of the family would attempt to hold him down, but when they failed to restrain him, Rachel sometimes sent for the manager or the police to put Alwyn safely in the lock-up for the night. The Peters' house, like so many on Weipa South, suffered badly as a result of these incidents. New boards patching up smashed glass louvres told of angry fists. Blood-stained floors were a visible reminder of the harm done to the person who began the rampage.

Alwyn left many blood-stains, not only when there was no meat for tea. Often, when he and Deidre fought, Alwyn would slash himself with a razor blade or a knife. Although Alwyn can remember the first time he cut himself (June 1979), he cannot recall what the fight was about. He does know that he was very drunk and furious with Deidre, and he remembers cutting his left arm with a razor blade.

A couple of weeks later Alwyn committed the same act again. On this occasion he was angry both at Deidre and his mother for chastising him because he drank too much. In this incident, Alwyn was so determined to mutilate himself after the chastisement, that Rachel was forced to call her nephews to take the blade from him.

His mother remembered another instance of Alwyn's anger, which in her own words, 'terrified me'. Rachel recalls Alwyn and Deidre returning home at about 2.00 p.m. after being at the canteen all morning. As usual they went into their room. A few minutes later an argument erupted and, according to Rachel, Deidre called out for help because Alwyn was cutting himself. Rachel attempted to take the blade from her son but Alwyn fought her off, turning over the table bearing all the Peters' food in the process. Blood dripped everywhere from Alwyn's arms and Rachel can remember fearing for his life. He recovered, but his arm still bears the scars.

Not only fights with Deidre or his mother caused Alwyn to mutilate himself. Sometimes, in an argument with his father Simon, Alwyn would deliberately mutilate himself rather than attack Simon. On one occasion in 1978, Alwyn, Simon and Rachel were very drunk and verbally abused each other. It appears that Simon and Rachel were fighting and Alwyn took the side of his mother. He became very upset and agitated, walked into the bush alone and he shot himself through the hand with a .22 rifle. Alwyn can remember the searing pain before lapsing into unconsciousness and waking up in a hospital bed, where stayed in for a month.

The thin line between channelling anger and hostility towards oneself and turning on loved ones is dramatically illustrated in the death of Deidre. Alwyn recalls the night of Deidre's death, when 'things went wrong': according to Alwyn, he had wanted to hurt himself, not Deidre.

Alwyn admitted he was drunk and jealous about Deidre; that he had a knife; that they argued violently. But he said he wanted to cut himself and would have done so if Deidre had not tried to intervene. Alwyn described the events this way:

> I was outside at the side of the house and I had the knife, because I wanted to cut myself. I don't remember what she said when she came out. She just came to stop me from cutting myself. She knew I wanted to cut myself because I told her in the lounge room I was going to cut myself. All I can remember about the knife is that I had the knife there. That was before I went out to cut myself.

Events may have happened as Alwyn described them. Deidre had frequently seen Alwyn cut himself and, with Rachel Peter, had tried to take knives away from him when he was drunk, so that he would not damage himself. Even on the night she was killed, Deidre, before the incident, took Alwyn's knife to Maggie Don to hide so that Alwyn would not cut himself again.

Alwyn remembers that Deidre, as so often in the past, had pleaded with him not to slash or stab himself. While Alwyn was outside his house, he said Deidre 'stopped me when I was outside by grabbing me by the arm and telling me not to do it. I don't remember how she got me inside . . . she took me (inside) by my left arm'.

Deidre was able to manoeuvre Alwyn into the house with Alwyn strongly resisting. In the ensuing struggle, she was killed. In Alwyn's words:

> I didn't try to hit her then, I kept pushing her away with my left hand until I got very angry with her, then I completely forgot about the knife I had in my hand and swung a punch at her and she fell back on the bed . . . when I turned to look for her she was lying on the bed. I saw blood on the side of her dress, I saw it from the light and realised I had stabbed her.

Alwyn used self-mutilation and violence towards others when frustrated, angry, or both. Which of these actions predominated appeared to depend, in part at least, on situational factors such as who was present at the time of conflict and how that person responded to Alwyn's confused state. But regardless of which action was taken, Alwyn's limited repertoire of defensive actions ensured that he or someone else was hurt, often very severely.

A Common Occurrence

Alwyn's acts of self-destruction are not exceptional. His adopted brother Raymond admitted to the same behaviour. According to Raymond:

> When I was drunk I dived through some glass louvres at our house. I went through head first. I was drunk. I think on this occasion I had been drinking whiskey. On another occasion when I had been drinking wine I came home and put my leg through the walls.

Such acts of self-destruction are not confined to the Peter family. Social worker Anne McKinnon compiled a list of people in Weipa South who were known to have committed acts of self-destruction. Her informants were the perpetrators or witnesses. The list below is incomplete but informative.

Name	Action
Clifford	Shot himself in thigh
Edward	Chopped arm with knife
Ernest	Hit louvres and died
Matthew	Hit louvres and died
Charles	Smashed louvres and died
Horace	(No details)
Edmund	Cut himself with razor blade
Ernest	Shot his hand
Cecil	Put hand through louvres
Dan	Cut his arm with knife
Robin	Cut himself with razor blade
Alwyn	Cut arm with razor blade
Ronnie	Cut himself with bread knife
Bruce	Cut himself with bottle
Amy	Smashed louvres
Sidney	Shot himself through hand
Alwyn	Shot himself through hand
Alwyn	Smashed louvres
Peter	Cut himself; chopped foot with axe
Andrew	Put hands through louvres
Stephen	Poured petrol on himself
Frank	Cut himself with axe
John	Punched louvres
Peter	Shot himself

These examples were obtained without much probing and were

The house of Percy from Edward River, who murdered his wife Annie.
The house has broken louvres — the result of punching or kicking them.

only recent cases widely known in the community. Detailed
accounts of the circumstances surrounding each incident are
lacking, but there is a very high frequency of self–mutilative acts
among males, at least on Weipa South.

However, some clues to the nature of these incidents come from
testimony gathered for use in Alwyn Peter's trial. Amy Peter, his
sister, frequently smashed louvres at the Peter household; her
hands still show the scars. According to Amy, 'I don't know why
I smash louvres when I am drunk and I feel that I don't know
what I am doing at the time'.

But Amy did have some insight into her behaviour. Later, in
her statement, she said, 'I don't think there was any way that I
could have released my anger other than by hitting the louvres'.
To demonstrate that self-mutilation is just an alternative to
hitting someone else, she candidly admits: 'When I am angry I
reach a point where I can't get rid of anger any other way besides
smashing things or getting stuck into somebody'.

Amy confirms what Alwyn's acts of self-mutilation suggest.
Violence towards oneself, as well as towards others, is spread

throughout Weipa South. According to Amy, not only do 'people have drunken fights every day at Weipa', but 'everybody I know reacts violently if something goes wrong in the house'. Amy should know: her boyfriend Allan often used a razor blade to cut his hands.

Even Ella Wymara, a gracious 66-year-old woman who can remember 'the good times' in Mapoon, has disturbing memories of her husband and the rest of her family regularly smashing louvre windows with their hands. These acts ceased only when tin louvres were fitted. As with Amy Peter, Ella Wymara does not really know why these actions occur, but she is sure that the self-destructive acts are 'not any part of our culture'.

The same picture of apparently purposeless violence is documented repeatedly by others on the reserve. Stephen, a school friend of Alwyn's, admitted that he 'goes silly when (he is) drunk' and he admits that he sometimes 'chases people with spears or a knife if (he doesn't) like them'. Even his own mother is not immune, for Stephen confessed that if he comes home drunk and there is no food ready, then he goes off his head and threatens his mother with sticks or a knife.

Stephen, as with so many others at Weipa, is especially prone to 'going funny' when tea or meat is not available; he punches louvres and often cuts himself so badly that he has to go to hospital. He says many friends of his (not on social worker Anne McKinnon's list) engage in the same action.

That relatively trivial actions are sufficient to motivate highly self-destructive acts can be seen in other instances Stephen gives. For example, he has one large scar across his right arm where he cut himself with a razor. According to Stephen, he committed the slash at the canteen because his mother refused to give him any money to buy cigarettes. On another occasion, Stephen slashed his arm with broken bottles and was admitted to hospital for treatment. His explanation for this act is disarmingly simple: 'I done it because my brother refused to drive me to the Albatross Hotel', he said.

Actions by other residents on reserves might not, on the surface, appear to be self-destructive, but on closer examination have an almost suicidal overtone to them. It is not uncommon for a young man to pick a losing fight with a much stronger and more experienced fighter. This often arises when the younger man is drunk and feeling guilty about something he has done. Observers have noted that this happens after abuse of a relative; beating a girlfriend; or when a man is unable to buy drinks in a 'grogging' group.

Social worker Matt Foley, in many years of experience working among Aboriginal people, has observed related behaviour. According to Foley, it is not unusual for Aborigines from reserve communities to grossly neglect serious injuries sustained in a brawl. 'They will', Foley said, 'simply lie down and do nothing'.

These practices are not confined to fights. Foley recounts his observations of a 13-year-old boy who regularly dug out the callouses on his feet with a knife until his soles bled profusely. The boy could give no explanation for his behaviour and Foley saw no apparent pattern in its occurrence.

Diverse motivations exist for self-destructive behaviour. Such actions as punching a fist through a louvre window, cutting oneself with a knife, or shooting a bullet through one's hand seem quite different from picking an unwinnable fight, or digging a knife into the soles of the feet — but the result is the same. These actions injure and scar those who engage in them.

These acts are not confined to Weipa South. Bill Rosser in his book, *This is Palm Island*, recounts another example. It appeared, according to Rosser, that the Queensland Department of Aboriginal and Islander Advancement decided that a Palm Island mother was unfit to care for her children. The children were moved by the Department to a children's dormitory, despite determined efforts by the mother to get them back. When she failed to obtain custody of her children, she poured kerosene over herself, set it alight and burned herself to death.

Such dramatic examples are probably exceptional, but other sources suggest that acts of self-destruction are widely known by health and welfare personnel working in official and unofficial capacities among reserve dwellers. Howard Stevens, a Queensland flying doctor, reported that 'self-mutilation was not uncommon' and also that attempted suicides were frequent on Queensland reserves. Stevens knew of at least five suicides and attempted suicides among black people on reserves and communities he visited in recent years, yet there were no instances of suicide among his white patients.

Although figures on suicide by reserve Aborigines are difficult to obtain, Stevens is convinced that this was a rare occurrence among traditional people — a view supported by experts such as psychiatrist Ivor Jones — and that far more occur than are officially recorded. Similarly, the high number of deaths caused by motor vehicle accidents among reserve dwellers requires further research. We documented 32 Aboriginal reserve dwellers who died in motor vehicle accidents between 1976 and 1980; many of these deaths were caused, according to one observer, by 'reckless . . . attempts by the driver to kill himself'.

John Taylor, an anthropologist at James Cook University, confirms Stevens' observations. Taylor, in preparing a report on dispute-settling procedures, discussed 'a veritable epidemic of suicide and self-mutilation in Aboriginal communities in North Queensland'. In attempting to explain this epidemic, Taylor suggested that Aborigines diverted rage and anger inward on themselves. He says, 'If they (Aborigines) were to attack the real objects of their anger, they would incur retribution from the Australian legal system'.

An Aboriginal welfare worker who often visits Queensland reserves has said: 'Aborigines cut themselves to get rid of anger and hostility at their inability to get a better deal from the government'. As with Taylor, this man had seen many examples of latent hostility caused by oppression. He recounted one case in which a man at Yarrabah hit his head against louvre windows until deep gashes appeared in the flesh. The self-mutilator had apparently been unable to persuade the white manager to part with money that the manager was holding in his name. The same welfare worker told of many other cases where frustration elicited by bureaucratic heavy-handedness — such as withholding social security payments and preventing relatives. from visiting reserves — manifested itself in punching fists through glass or walls, or gashing of hands or body.

White administrators know of these acts but are reluctant to discuss them publicly. However, John Goodin, manager of Weipa South reserve, gave a statement to Peter Clapin of the Public Defender's office about Alwyn Peter's history at the reserve. In his statement, Goodin pointed to the prevalence of self-mutilative acts: 'There are quite a few instances of people committing acts of self-mutilation in the community. Often the Aborigines shoot themselves in the hands or feet'. Goodin said he thought Aborigines may do this because 'they are looking for sympathy'.

Goodin's explanation for the acts of self-mutilation is, however, unduly simplistic. Alwyn, for example, rarely sought assistance after he cut or shot himself and, indeed, had an abhorrence of hospitals. Many of his self-destructive exploits, and those of this friends, were carried out at the height of anger and frustration. The slashes and cuts were spontaneous, rather than premeditated, suggesting that no account was taken of the response of others.

This does not preclude the possibility that sometimes self-destructive deeds occur to seek the attention of others. Various motivations are possible for recent self-mutilative behaviour, just as in traditional society such behaviour occurred under a variety of social stimuli. The question is, however, whether present behaviour reflects the practices of the past.

Old Customs

Self-inflicted injuries in traditional Aboriginal society were often part of rituals, practised during mourning, initiation, or before a battle. These practices varied considerably from one part of the continent to another, but the frequency of the acts suggest that mutilation was a mark of high maturity in traditional culture.

Among the Arunta tribes of central Australia, bloodletting was common in magical ceremonies for the increase of the totemic animals and plants of the regions. Thus, in order to multiply emus, the men of the tribe cleared a small area of level ground, opened the veins in their arms and allowed the blood to soak into the earth. Similar ceremonies existed to make the Hakea tree burst into blossom and assist in the multiplication of kangaroos.

It is highly unlikely that any of the incidents of self-destruction occurring on Queensland reserves have any resemblance to traditional food-multiplication practices. But some traditional methods of showing bereavement are similar to current practices among Aborigines. Traditional methods varied from one tribe to another. Among the tribes of the River Darling, mourning men stood by the open grave and cut each other's heads with a boomerang. Holding their bleeding heads over the grave they allowed the blood to drip on the corpse at the bottom of it.

More pertinently, perhaps, at the Vasse River in Western Australia, before a body was lowered into the grave, Aborigines gashed their thighs. In Queensland many tribes slashed their bodies or foreheads to show sorrow at the death or injury of a kin, a practice that still occurs today. Anthropologist David Trigger reports that, at Doomadgee, a woman hearing news of her son's injuries would have slashed herself had David not been present. Such practices are still common among older Aborigines in remote areas of Queensland, and, although not emulated by the young, are rituals that are at least respected by many of them. Even in the city, Aborigines occasionally display similar behaviour. In Archie Weller's novel, *The Day of the Dog*, the hero, a young Aboriginal man called Doug, discusses friendship with his mate Floyd. During the conversation Floyd tells Doug that he would 'hurt himself if you was killed Doug. I like you that much.'

In traditional times blood-letting was used in a variety of other circumstances. The aged and the sick received blood from others, and a young man often would open a vein in his arm and let the fluid trickle over the body of an older man in order to strengthen his aged friend. Similarly, among the Warramunga tribe and the Kalkadoons, the old men drew blood from their own subincised penises in the presence of young adolescents who a few days before had undergone the operation of subincision. The object of this custom was to promote the healing of the young men's wounds. But in Queensland, these practices are now virtually non-existent.

Self-mutilation has traditionally been associated with violence and aggression. The Warramunga men often fought among themselves with blazing torches and while fighting, the women burnt themselves with lighted twigs in the belief that by doing so they prevented the men from inflicting serious injury on each other. Some Queensland tribes in the past cut themselves and dipped their spears in their own blood before engaging in battle. In the Wiimbaio tribe in the south-east of the country, if a man nearly killed his wife in rage, the woman was laid out on the ground and the veins of her husband opened allowing blood to flow onto the woman's body. The intention was apparently to restore her to life by means of the blood drawn from her assailant.

More macabre ceremonies mark the association of blood and violence. For example, in central Australia, before an avenging party started out to take the life of a distant enemy, all the men stood up, opened veins in their genital organs with sharp flints or pointed sticks, and allowed the blood to spurt over each other's thighs. The ceremony was supposed to create mutual strength and knit them so closely together that treachery became impossible.

Little of the self-mutilation and violence described in this book, however, bears any relationship to the traditional forms of mutilation for bereavement, ritual and group cohesiveness in battle. Frustration, aggression and alcohol are the hallmarks of contemporary self-mutilation. Both the old and the new forms of self-destruction have the common elements of stress underlying them, but the nature of the stress varies greatly. Bereavement and initiation into adulthood are clearly full of tension and anxiety. It could be argued that minor frustrations such as being insulted at a grogging party or coming home drunk and not finding any meat for dinner are also stressful, but the analogy is weak and should not be pushed too far.

Not surprisingly, most of the parents and grandparents of those who cut themselves denied that these violent acts had any traditional origins. To them, the act of deliberately cutting oneself as a mark of respect for the dead is far removed from spontaneously slashing one's arms because of anger felt towards a partner. But even so, there may be some slight connections. Most of the young people on reserves knew and respected their elders' symbolic acts of showing sorrow by self-inflicted wounds.

The very visibility of a bereavement cut demonstrates to the world that hurt has occurred and stress has been experienced. Others can see that a bereaved person is suffering and, if they wish, empathise with the sufferer. So it is, perhaps, with a contemporary self-mutilator. Frustration and anger are felt by those who hurt themselves and the wounds bear testimony to others that these emotions are being experienced.

It is possible, therefore, that a modelling effect has taken place and that there is a link between the past and the present. Younger people may have copied ancient practices of dealing with stress — such as cutting oneself — and applied them to the quite different circumstances existing on reserves.

There are parallels with traditional practices and violence towards others on reserves. In traditional society, it was reasonable to inflict specific punishment on a man who had aggrieved another. So, Ivor Jones has demonstrated, among the Warburton Range Aborigines, ritualised spearing often occurs. But the spear is always aimed at a particular part of the body, in most cases the thigh, and disputes end when an injury occurs. In fact, over a 10-year period, Jones discovered only one death and one severe injury resulting in amputation. This contrasts with the forms of violence discussed in this book. For in self-mutilation and violence against others, randomness and spontaneity characterise the attacks.

Current violent practices are hardly symbolic acts with sacramental qualities and functions. They are acts performed under stress, but they derive from low self-esteem and a sense of futility in life. They are acts which, as the renowned anthropologist, Professor Stanner, has so perceptively put it, are indices of the contempt Aborigines feel towards themselves:

I consider that the extent of self-injury is possibly a measure of the Aboriginal sense of inability to re-establish a life of self-esteem. Our relations with them are power-relations; their situation is one of complete dependence and acceptance, which to many is hateful in their tradition and hurtful to their pride. Many have complained to me, and have used the metaphor of cattle yarded, so that they turn this way or that, and try as they will, they can find no exit.

Stanner points out that to give blood freely and generously was regarded as a mark of high maturity among traditional people. But 'to damage oneself to the point of incapacitation was not — to the best of my knowledge — part of the mentality or motivation of the act'.

Alwyn and all the others who mutilated themselves were frustrated, feeling stressed and full of self-contempt. They had, according to psychiatrist Harry Eastwell, 'few things to give them a source of self-esteem or positive feelings about themselves'. Referring to Alwyn specifically, Eastwell pointed out in his trial evidence that this aggressive drive often turned towards himself — not considering himself a person of worth, he shot or cut himself.

Although frustration and aggression lie behind the acts of self-destruction it is quite possible, as we have seen, that the injuries sustained serve other functions as well. A cut on the body can be a sign to others that one has been deeply hurt emotionally by a loved one. Alwyn, for example, was emotionally scarred by Deidre's liaisons with other men. But in contrast to traditional society, no social sanctions were available to Alwyn to punish her behaviour or acknowledge her wronging of him. So Alwyn mutilated himself as an expression of this hurt. Similarly, it is very possible that when Alwyn shot himself in the hand he was attempting to stop the argument raging between his parents. This self-scapegoating act is a device often used by people to maintain the immediate social system around them. As with the occurrence of self-mutilation in maximum security prisons, self-inflicted gashes and wounds may give young Aboriginal men status and prestige among their peers.

But frustration and anger recur as the underlying causes of self-mutilation. We know from studies of suicide that frustration of any sort produces feelings of hostility which are often manifested in aggressive acts. Further, these studies suggests that aggressive acts need not be directed at the source of the frustration but instead can be channelled against one-self or towards another convenient target. Alwyn directed this aggression in both ways — he mutilated himself and he injured others.

Such frustrations do not seem to have existed in traditional society. Psychiatrist Ivor Jones searched for instances of suicide in traditional Aboriginal communities and found that such acts were impossible to uncover. When suicides were found, 'every instance was one where the traditional way had broken down'.

The breakdown of traditional society has also contributed to the frustrations and stresses experienced by both men and women in Aboriginal communities. The research material has led me to believe that men manifest their frustration and anger in self-mutilative acts. But what of the women?

Although the cases in the dossiers and the accounts by residents of life on reserves give only one example (Amy Peter) of female self-mutilation, anthropologists and others have confirmed that such cases do occur, but with far less frequency than with male self-injury.

Does this mean that women find life less stressful or less frustrating than men, or that they display their frustrations and stress in other ways? Without a full-scale observational study, this question is almost impossible to answer. However, some tentative suggestions emerge from present evidence. To begin with, although I suspect that women cope with everyday life on reserves better than men, both sexes have frustration and stress levels that are far higher than for most whites. The morbidity figures discussed in Chapter 6 demonstrate this point.

Women may have lost their traditional forms of power and prestige in contemporary communities — an argument cogently expressed by Bell and Ditton — but they appear to manage or adapt better than males to their social context. Fewer women than men drink heavily; not as many appear as aimless and disoriented, and fewer mutilate themselves. On the positive side, many women are powerful voices on community councils and negotiate with white authority more easily than their menfolk.

However, as with men, the response of women to the frustrations of reserve life varies from one age group to another, and from one area to another. On some reserves, observers report that women often fight among themselves and have higher rates of mental illness than men. In other communities, the most frustrated and angry group of Aborigines is teenage girls, who are attracted to the music and life-style of white culture but find the gap between it and their current existence almost overwhelming. However, until specific research is carried out in these areas we are left with conjecture.

What is certain, however, is that in contrast to middle-class whites, who usually learn to deal with stress and frustration in socially accepted ways, reserve Aborigines often resort to violence. But this violence, directed towards oneself or displaced onto someone else, had its origins with whites. When the dreamtime disintegrated, when whites broke, possibly forever, the link between the past, present and future, hopelessness and desperation became endemic in Aboriginal community life.

4 Death of the Dreamtime

Life Before Whites

Captain James Cook, at times a perceptive observer of human affairs, was one of the few early white men who realised that the values and beliefs of Europeans were not those that should be used in evaluating native peoples. In his *Journal*, he said:

> They may appear to be the most wretched people upon the earth, but in reality, they are far more happier than we Europeans being wholly unacquainted not only with the superfluous but the necessary conveniences so much sought after in Europe, they are happy in not knowing the use of them. They live in a tranquility not disturbed by the inequality of condition.

The famous explorer might well have unduly romanticised the 'tranquility' of traditional society — it could, in the words of one Aborigine, be short, nasty and brutal — but at least he did not denigrate their entire mode of existence.

Such perceptiveness was singularly lacking among other early observers of Aborigines. One commentator in 1847 suggested that:

> regret concerning the disappearance (of the Aborigine) is hardly more reasonable than it would be to complain of drainage of marshes or the disappearance of wild animals.

Attempts to comprehend the beliefs and values of the indigenous people were generally couched in Western terms. Thus the land, the very soul of Aboriginal existence, was conceptualised within Anglo-Saxon conventions of private property and cultivation. The prevailing view of the settlers was that because the Aborigines were a nomadic people and did not grow crops, it did not matter if they were moved from one area to another. Even Cook believed that because Aborigines did not cultivate the soil, they were inhabitants but not proprietors of the land.

However, the land had a vitally different meaning for Aborigines. To them the land was created and peopled in the Dreamtime by super-humans. These became features of the landscape as well as ancestors to the inhabitants. Aboriginal rights to the land were therefore as old as the landscape itself, so that the land and people were intimately linked and to remove one from the other was to commit spiritual homicide.

White adults could not comprehend what Aboriginal children knew from an early age: that the land cemented the past to the present, determining the relationship of one person with another. Ceremonies, sealing the relationship between Aborigines, the land, clans and tribes, ensured that all people were aware of their place in the community and in the universe. Despite differences between one tribe and another, every native Australian recognised the importance of the land and of the tribes that occupied it.

Alwyn Peter's ancestors, the people of the Mapoon region, were typical. The tribes in an area divided up their land according to specific geographical features, in this case the river system. The clans of Alwyn's tribe, the Tjungundji, took their names from the territories they occupied. The territorial position of a clan relative to other clans gave a group its identity. The people of the tribe inherited a special relationship with the land through their grandfathers. The totemic values of the land and the kinship structure gave people specific positions in their communities.

Neighbouring clans of different tribes often had more in common with each other than two distant clans of the same tribe. For example, the neighbouring Mapoon clans of the Tjungundji and Yupungatti tribes were united through their relationships with the totemic places. These tribes intermarried, but complex rules governed who could marry. A girl went to her husband at puberty, and if her husband died, the deceased's brother would assume responsibility for her.

The land and the sea provided the Mapoon people with all they needed. When water was scarce, the people sank wells or tapped water-bearing trees. Major sources of food such as fish, marine life, birds, animals and wild vegetables were abundant, and various cooking methods such as roasting, leaching, boiling or grilling were developed, with special processes for removing toxins. Well developed bush medicines were used to treat injuries

(Alwyn's father, Simon Peter, still treats poisonous snake-bites with these medicines).

The Mapoon people's dispute-settling processes were essentially self-redressive. They laid a heavy burden on the individual to conduct his own case, whether in prosecution of a wrong action or in defending himself when charged. Punishments often appeared, by our standards, to be severe, but they were accepted by the people. Spearing and banishments from a tribe were common methods of dealing with individuals who broke personal, cultural or spiritual rules but, as discussed below, these punishments were appropriate forms of social control.

Group disputes involving territorial violations were settled in specific ways. If an intruding person or group was found, men from the tribe cut themselves about their chests and arms, placed blood on the tips of their spears and faced the intruders. If the interlopers acknowledged their trespass, a confrontation might be minimised by one intruder offering his leg or thigh for spearing. But if no acknowledgement of the trespass occurred, a full scale feud could develop.

There were no rulers or chiefs of the Mapoon tribes, but men and women knew their specific places in the community. When a man reached old age, the elders of the community shared secrets and myths with him. With other elders, he became the repository of the tribe's wisdom and knowledge. These men, in forming loosely organised councils, made many of the decisions of the clans. Women also had their sources of power — centred on the gathering of food, ceremonial functions and child-raising — which have largely disappeared today.

For the Mapoon people, life was ordered, rich in social experiences and highly spiritual. The Dreamtime united people to the land and determined the values that were immutably rooted in the past. Money, the accumulation of material wealth, alcohol and white technology were all unknown.

The squatters and missionaries changed all this. With a desire for land and a zeal for religious conversion, they transformed the face of traditional society. Much violence accompanied this change, and the Mapoon elders remember the process well. Mrs Jean Jimmy, in recounting the history of her people, talked of the cattlemen Lachlan Kennedy and Frank Jardine, who were 'the first whites to settle the area. According to Jean Jimmy, 'they were killing people all the way up. At Dingle Dingle Creek they killed most of the tribe'.

Frank Don, Harry Toeboy and many other Mapoon elders tell

the tales of murder and massacre that were faithfully recounted to them by their parents. At Seven River, for example, white settlers hid in trees and shot any Aborigine they could see. The accounts describe how Jardine killed black children by knocking their heads against trees, and how he and Kennedy together exterminated hundreds of Aborigines.

The government, the missionaries and the pastoralists continued to take people from their homes. A concerted drive was made to have the children of white fathers and black mothers abducted by the police, and those stolen in north Queensland were sent to Mapoon or Palm Island. The latter became a receiving area for dispersed peoples, including survivors from the Kalkadoon tribe.

The missionaries, although generally not guilty of slaughter, prostituted Aboriginal spiritual and cultural values and, in the words of the World Council of Churches, 'took a part in the destruction of Aboriginal culture and institutions'. The Presbyterians, for example, began their mission at Mapoon in 1898, and then systematically dismantled all that the Mapoon people held sacred.

Mrs Jean Jimmy remembers that before the mission there were many tribes, but 'the missionaries took us into the dormitory at the age of three years old and there we had to learn to speak like our mission ladies'. She also remembers the missionaries indoctrinating them with Christianity, forcing them to learn English, discouraging the use of native languages and teaching them 'how to be moral'. Her mother, however, knew something of the tribe and its culture and tried to teach Jean Jimmy her native language and history.

The missionaries saw their role as constructive. As they tell their tale in *The Mapoon Story*, their mission attempted to save the Aborigines from the more brutal white settlers. The Presbyterians also argued that their decision to close down the mission originated in 1958 when they became concerned about the inaccessibility of the area and the lack of work. However, these excuses are not the reasons the mission closed; rather, the Aborigines believe, the Church, the Government and the Comalco company worked hand-in-hand to expel them from their home so that the land could be mined.

The sequence of events that eventually led to the closure of the mission in 1963 probably began in 1957, when negotiations between Comalco and the Queensland Government led to a proposal to mine bauxite in the area. The Act which followed provided for a lease of 2270 square miles of Aboriginal reserve land on the west coast of Cape York, from which the mining company was required to select and retain an area of 1000 square miles for a minimum of 105 years. This lease also provided the company with all timber, cattle-grazing, water and farming rights. It was clearly no coincidence that the Weipa and Mapoon missions were both in the area leased by the company.

Between 1957 and 1963, there were numerous discussions between the Church, the company and the State Government on what should be done with the missions. As a result of these discussions, it was decided that the Weipa settlement would remain, but Mapoon would be closed down. The people at Mapoon were to be moved away. The Church, the Government and the company made sure the move occurred, and the Aborigines remember exactly how this happened.

The Process of Destruction

In a succession of swift developments, changes occurred at Mapoon which affected everyone on the mission. In 1963, a much-disliked missionary, called by the people 'Mr Whiteman', suddenly left the settlement. Then the flying doctor service to the mission was suspended, closely followed by the discontinuation of the supply boat to Mapoon, which led to the closure of the local store.

Meanwhile, according to Rachel Peter, 'our church people and the Assistant Director of Aboriginal Affairs, Killoran, came and said the bulldozers will come and dig up all our homes — and will dig holes over all our hunting grounds and we will have nothing left'. Although the bulldozers did not come, other events followed which were equally threatening. The local school was closed. Then, in the most dramatic event of the Mapoon story, a government boat arrived at the mission on the night of 15 November 1963, carrying both white and native police. The police went from house to house ordering the people to pack their bags and to sleep, under guard, at the mission cottage.

One of the first houses the police went to was occupied by Robert Reid, who remembers vividly what happened: 'I looked up and asked "Are you a policeman?". He said "Yea". I asked him, "Why have you come?". He replied, "To shift you people". I said to him, "Give me the reason". He said, "Well, I have no reason to give but this has been our word from Mr Killoran".'

The next day the government boat, *Gelam*, left with five families aboard for Janie Creek to round up more Mapoon people. Among those herded on board were Alwyn's grandparents. Frank and Maggie Don recalled that as the government boat approached Janie Creek children could be heard crying from inside the hulls.

Despite the closing-down of the school and the store, the Peter family and 40 other people were determined to stay at the settlement. All miscalculated, however, the determination of the white man to remove them from their land.

Shortly after *Gelam* left, carpenters employed by the Department of Native Affairs arrived at Mapoon and carried out an act of aggression that symbolised, to the Mapoon people, the whites' behaviour towards them. As Rachel Peter recalls, nearly everything on the mission was burnt down, including homes, church, cookhouse, school, workshops, butcher-shop and store.

Rachel saw the Department's carpenters 'going to the coconut trees, getting dry coconut branches, putting it under the homes and into the homes and striking a match'. The destruction of Mapoon was virtually complete. Armed police, forced transportation and arson were the weapons used to solve the problems of Comalco, the Church and the Government.

But the Peters' love of the area drew them back to Mapoon. Year after year, Rachel, Simon, Alwyn and the others returned to their traditional home to hunt and fish. They set up a small hut and explored the land they knew so well. These visits, however, were only a few months long because they always had to travel back to Weipa for supplies. Travel between the two areas was difficult.

The psychological effects of these events on Alwyn and his family should not be under-estimated. Jean Jimmy records: 'When you are burning down a home it means you burn the whole body of our Aboriginal custom, and they die so fast... I have seen since the removal of Mapoon how people just died away after the burning down of our homes'.

Although Alwyn was only eight when the police took his grandparents away and white bureaucrats burnt down the houses at Mapoon, the effect would have been profound. Alwyn's love of the area was intense, and he and his relatives frequently referred to Mapoon as though it was their only home.

Alwyn recalled his childhood days in the area as basically happy. It is true that he remembers with some degree of discomfort the beatings he received from his mother and father when he was bad. But he remembers with pleasure playing with other boys at Mapoon, swimming, using a spear, and learning hunting and fishing skills from his father. Despite the occasional beating from his parents, Alwyn was surrounded by devoted and loving relatives. Maggie Don, his grandmother, was especially

Maggie, the grandmother of Alwyn Peter, with two of her great grand-children at Weipa South.

close to him and in her own words would 'grow Alwyn up' when his mother was sick or absent.

Alwyn's love of Mapoon, as with that of his other relatives, was genuine and intense. Alwyn told social worker Matt Foley: 'I have love for my father's ground, because it is my father's tribal ground and I respect it'. Foley says Alwyn often referred to tribal legends associated with this land and commented on how he had felt less lonely when he was at Mapoon. Contrasting his love for the land with his love for women, Alwyn said, simply but poignantly, 'I love the land more than I love the girl'.

His love of Mapoon certainly was reflected in his behaviour. Relatives and friends testified that Alwyn would hunt and fish with skill and finesse, meet his friends without fighting them, and display a tranquillity of spirit that was never displayed at Weipa. These changes were particularly noticeable when the Peters returned to Mapoon for short stays after their resettlement at Weipa.

Rachel Peter, as with her son, also found living much easier in her traditional homelands. She found Alwyn a 'different boy' at Mapoon, and contrasted his tranquil and sober mood with the morose, aggressive and frequently drunken youth she saw at Weipa. Rachel was also happy because there was an abundance of traditional food in the area, such as yams, crayfish, oysters, sea turtles, ducks and geese. All these were a welcome relief from the white menu of meat and rice consumed daily at Weipa South.

The Peters were content at Mapoon because, in the words of Jean Jimmy, 'the land is most important to we Aborigines. It is sacred of us, in our customs'. Alwyn wished to follow many of his relatives and friends who returned to Mapoon, and told Mr Justice Dunn during his trial that when he had received his punishment from the court he would go back to his father's land.

Throughout Queensland, the Mapoon story was repeated as Aborigines were forced off their land and resettled elsewhere. Palm Island people are now known as the 'Bwgcolmans'. This, the name of the original inhabitants of Palm Island, was adopted by all the Aborigines who were removed to the Island. Those from the Island and from other places in the State remember with some bitterness their forced removal from one area to another.

Aboriginal activist Shorty O'Neil and his mother lived at Rose Bay in Townsville for many years. However, when the local authorities decided to make Rose Bay an elite suburb, bulldozers came in and cleared all the makeshift houses in the area. O'Neil recalls that he and his mother were living in an air-raid shelter which proved to be too strong for the bulldozers. According to O'Neil, about three years after the bulldozers came, he and his mother were in town for the day and there was no one in the shelter. On returning, they found the shelter bricked up with all their belongings still inside. Later, O'Neil says, 'we busted some of the bricks out to get the belongings, and then some people moved back in there'. However, when the people went out one day, 'they (the authorities) came and put iron plating sheets over the doors where we busted the bricks so nobody could live there'.

These incidents illustrate the destruction of Aboriginal society. Their effects on individuals, families and tribes were considerable, and it is remarkable that even some elements of Aboriginality survived the white invasion.

Aboriginality: What is Left?

'Aboriginality' is a term that should not be defined by referring only to traditional ways of life. For, as Marcia Langton, an Aboriginal researcher, has trenchantly pointed out, the pervading popular assumption that urban Aborigines have been assimilated into the white population and adopted white life-styles is doubtful to say the least.

Despite the inability of researchers to study urban Aboriginal society without recourse to Western concepts of poverty — a term not known in traditional communities — some evidence suggests that distinctive Aboriginal ways of doing things exist even in cities. Dynamic adaptation to white ways has made kinship systems and family structures different from traditional patterns but still distinctively Aboriginal.

Thus, in cities such as Brisbane, which receives many families from reserves in the north of the State, 'matrifocal' family structures are common. In a matrifocal family, women effectively become the leaders and decision-makers of the unit, even if men are present. In contrast to the past, when men were the undisputed leaders of the community, males in towns are often unable to take command. Unemployment, itinerant labour patterns, imprisonment and regulations relating to social security payments for supporting mothers, often force the men away from their homes, effectively placing women in charge.

Even on Queensland reserves, matrifocal family patterns often occur. Many of Alwyn's female relatives, such as Maggie Don, Rachel Peter and Ella Wymara, are forceful women. They are highly respected and influence family life as much, if not more, than the men do.

These examples provide ample evidence to demonstrate that both on and off reserves, basic family patterns have been severely distorted by white contact. Adaptation by men and women to this contact is neither creative nor rewarding. For example, Alwyn's female relatives repeatedly expressed horror at the incidence of violent abuse and rape they were subjected to by their men. In the past, women would have been protected by the web of relationships which ensured that relatives would intercede if a man treated his wife badly. This network has broken down, as the incidence of violent crime demonstrates.

Women suffer abuse in other ways as well. In traditional society, women had autonomy in ritual domains, such as crisis-of-life ceremonies, and in food gathering and preparation. But with births occurring in hospitals, first menstruations in school, and money and packaged foods increasingly becoming units of exchange, much of this power and autonomy is lost.

In our study of Queensland reserves, and in Bell and Ditton's research in central Australia, Aboriginal women complained that they had lost the basis of economic independence with the loss of land over which to forage. Many Aboriginal women also said that they did not receive the money which men were paid for themselves and their dependents. Some pointed to instances in which men became violent when social security payments left little for buying alcohol or meat. Cases of men assaulting their wives and girlfriends for these reasons often occur on Queensland reserves.

Women have suffered as a result of the white conquest, but so have men. Imprisonment, illness and early death through violence depletes the number of males able to act as community leaders. Many men complain that in order to have any income at all they must leave the reserves and seek employment elsewhere, whereas the welfare dollar comes directly to women. Men, rather than women, obtain positions on reserve councils, but these are ultimately run by white managers and the Department of Aboriginal and Islander Advancement. This negates their power in comparison with former times.

Family relationships have also changed markedly. Traditional marriage ceremonies are becoming less popular, being increasingly replaced by de facto relationships. Polygyny, the practice of having more than one wife, so strongly featured in traditional society, is all but gone, and the system of 'promises' is not much more than a memory. The impermanent nature of de facto relationships is frequently used by women to remind men that they are only living together. Indeed many of the victims of violence that we studied left their men or had liaisons with others. In short, relationships previously structured by well defined rights and obligations are now fragile and often short-term affairs.

Rape, virtually unknown in traditional society, appears to be a common occurrence on some reserves today. However, its reporting rate is clearly low as not one case was discovered in our dossiers. This apparent acceptance of rape, with a reluctance to report the crime to white authorities, ensures that few cases ever reach a criminal court. but many Aboriginal women expressed to me their strong disapproval and fear of sexual assault.

Love of children is still strong in contemporary Aboriginal communities. However, alcohol and high levels of frustration and stress ensure that beatings and cruelty towards offspring occur — far more often, it seems, than in traditional times. Alwyn received severe beatings from both his parents, although in most other cases that came to my attention, the father administered most of the unjustified beatings.

Elderly people do not receive the same respect as they did in the past, particularly as the elected council system operating in many Aboriginal communities cuts across traditional ways, when elders were the community leaders. The extended family is still prevalent in Queensland reserves, but the incidence of violence and abuse within the family has diminished its cohesion and effectiveness.

The coming of white man has brought great changes and disruption to established patterns of Aboriginal life. The displacement of native people from their clans and land has deprived a deeply religious people of their continuity with the past and the future, and has removed their means of subsistence. These changes have severely affected the nature of power relationships within Aboriginal families and groups.

Despite obvious differences from one part of the State to another, a depressing monoculture pervades Aboriginal society. This culture is based on uncertain wages, habitual welfare handouts, unstable family life, and violence. Alcohol, perhaps the greatest destroyer of community life, darkens this gloomy picture and is increasingly being used by both the very young and the very old. As one black woman told former Weipa South Manager, Don Egan, 'well, if I'm going to be beaten up it doesn't hurt so much if I'm drunk'.

The lack of variety within much of Aboriginal culture has a harmful effect on young and old. The young either succumb to the ways of their elders and drink and gamble heavily, or turn to white 'pop' culture with its emphasis on rock music, flashy clothes and fast cars. Young girls, emulating the Hollywood images they see in cinemas or on television screens, often become obsessed with romantic love. But the love they find on the reserves is very different from the painless and comfortable emotion portrayed by Brooke Shields or Tatum O'Neal.

Older people also become depressed by the dull negativism of reserve existence. With their men constantly drunk and with violence around them all the time, older women often try desperately to stop the destructive behaviour. What is known on some reserves as the 'tut-tut' brigade — a group of older women — admonish their men for their excessive drinking, fighting and what they see as general apathy. But they face insurmountable hurdles in changing patterns of behaviour, and recent reports of heavy drinking among older people would suggest that some have given up hope themselves. So, without acceptable alternative role-models, young and old see few opportunities for substantial social change.

Not all of the past has been lost. The love of the land remains firmly planted in most Aborigines' minds. The desire for self-determination and self-control is also abundantly clear. Positive community life, although very different from the past, exists in some areas, where strong extended family networks ensure that children are brought up in a warm and affectionate environment. Although the pursuit of material possessions, such as cars and television sets, often emulates that of whites, private property does not hold the importance that it does in white societies, and communal sharing of resources is still greater than can be seen among white Australians.

Strong Aboriginal men and women still work on communities and constantly remind people that there are other ways of living besides those shown by status-conscious whites. Increasingly, writers such as Archie Weller and Aboriginal author Kevin Gilbert remind blacks and whites that there is a distinctive Aboriginal way of looking at life. In short, the seeds of Aboriginality remain, germinating in most black communities despite the white invasion and the influx of drugs and material goods.

All of this may not be the Dreamtime as it was known, but as

Stanner has observed, there is at least some evidence that the people are 'exploring a potential of their structure, (and) taking advantage of its flexibility'. Such advantage will never be fully realised, however, until part of the contemporary Aboriginal culture — alcohol — is effectively controlled.

5 White Man's Drugs

Violence and Alcohol

Throughout this book, one commodity has been repeatedly linked with the criminal violence and self-mutilation that characterises most Aboriginal communities. The white man's drug, alcohol, has from the moment of settlement, been both deliberately and unwittingly used to fragment community life. From the time the early settlers exchanged alcohol for the sexual favours of black women, to the time money was given for work performed and used to buy drink, drunkenness and alcoholism have enslaved native Australians.

The most dramatic and worrying statistic, from the analysis of the cases of violence recorded, related to alcohol. It was found that in 95 per cent of homicides and serious assaults, alcohol in large quantities was directly involved. In more than 50 per cent of these cases, both offender and victim had been drinking. White Australians have a culture of drinking — the 'mateship' syndrome reinforces heavy consumption — but the association between crime and alcohol does not seem to be as great as in Aboriginal society.

When the levels of alcohol involved in the cases of Aboriginal violence were classified, it was quite clear that the drinking was not of a mild or sociable kind. The Commonwealth Department of Health published a detailed report in 1979 which included a classification of drinking habits. When we looked at the amount of alcohol our violent offenders said they had consumed before the offence — always a conservative estimate — it was apparent that the levels were very high.

From the Health Department's report, we ascertained that 30 per cent of offenders had been drinking 'heavily' before the attack and 60 per cent had been drinking 'very heavily'. In only two of the 82 cases we analysed was there no record of alcohol consumption. Given the lack of detail in the dossiers and the limitation of information — about duration of drinking, number of people bringing alcohol along to a party, and actual intake — I believe that the figures above are a gross under-estimation of the amount of alcohol consumed by offenders.

Many cases contained descriptions of drinking habits that added flesh to these bare statistical skeletons. A man, who eventually killed his wife, drank six jugs in the two hours before attacking her; another admitted to consuming 'at least 18 bottles of beer that night'; another young man, charged with unlawful wounding, described the day he attacked his girlfriend this way:

> At ten o'clock I took five big bottles of beer to a friend's house, drank them, at one o'clock I had another two bottles of beer and then we started to play cards. Later we consumed three flagons of wine during the afternoon.

Alwyn Peter admitted to having been 'very drunk' at the time of killing Deidre and had in the hours preceding the stabbing, consumed huge quantities of beer, wine and what he called 'hot-stuff', meaning rum. All the other offenders previously discussed had consumed vast quantities of alcohol.

The dynamics involved in pre-violence drinking sessions can be seen in the case of Duncan, a 31-year-old man from Aurukun, charged with two counts of unlawful wounding. Duncan, a married man with three children, stabbed his brother Stuart, and a mutual friend Saul, with a pocket knife.

The reasons for the attacks are obscure to all the participants, but, as with many similar instances, offender and victim described themselves as 'very good friends'. That this statement had some basis in reality can be seen by the fact that Duncan turned up at court to face the unlawful wounding charges heavily inebriated as a result of sharing reconciliation drinks with one of the victims.

It appears that the attacks occurred during a 'blackfellows drinking party'. No one knew exactly how much alcohol was con-sumed, but at least four cartons of beer and four flagons of wine were drunk by those present. Saul, one of the victims, said they had had quite a few beers and were talking when Duncan started 'talking louder and then he started yelling and Stuart, his older brother, said to him, "Duncan keep quiet, the police will come".'

According to Saul, Duncan stood up and pulled out a black pocket knife. Duncan and Stuart 'were arguing real fierce like and it looked like they were going to have a fight, so I stood up and tried to stop them'. Saul then pushed the two combatants away from each other and said to Duncan, 'You can't fight your own brother. Don't be stupid.' Duncan replied by saying, 'Get out the fucking way before I stab you.'

He then stabbed both Saul and Stuart, who ran away. Duncan, when arrested by the police admitted being 'really drunk' but said he just wanted to pass the knife to his brother 'because I might cut myself'.

Yet another case, that of Lloyd, illustrates the typical elements in alcohol-related violence. Lloyd, a Hopevale reserve resident, attempted to kill his uncle with a gun after a heavy drinking session that had led to a brawl. Lloyd was not sure about how the brawl started. He carried a gun because he had a severe liver disease which had left him weak and unable to defend himself. His uncle and he had fought while drunk in the past, and Lloyd, physically inferior to his uncle, resorted to a gun 'to defend himself' in this incident.

Lloyd's history of drinking began at the age of 16. He said he drank to forget his miseries and because he 'had nothing to look forward to in life'. His father, his other relatives and most of his friends had severe drinking problems. He said he drank till he was completely drunk and had done this frequently. As a result, he had severe liver disease and at the age of 25 had a medical prognosis of dying at 30 if he continued drinking. Lloyd was not lacking in insight: he strongly felt that the whites and the introduction of alcohol had deflected Aborigines from their old ways and destructively changed the nature of black communities.

Both cases illustrate typical characteristics of the alcohol-triggered aggression that is almost a daily occurrence on many Aboriginal reserves. For, as in the case of Duncan, a party begins with friends and relatives in a convivial setting. Then large amounts of alcohol are drunk over relatively short periods of time and suddenly the mood of the group changes.

In both Duncan's and Lloyd's case, mood changes were precipitated very easily. A word out of place, an implied insult or a slight disagreement on any issue was often a sufficient reason for a friend to become an enemy and a much-loved relative a hated foe.

Both Duncan and Lloyd had only hazy recollections about the reasons for their fights, and in Duncan's case, the participants quickly forgave each other shortly after the incident finished. But in these cases, as in many others, the period between the alleged insult and its forgotten memory explodes into violent confrontation. In Duncan's incident, he thought about cutting himself but instead, for reasons he cannot remember, cut someone else.

Heavy Aboriginal drinkers are typically suffering bad health. Of male Aborigines who reach the age of 20, one in five will be dead by 40, compared with one in 29 for the total male population of Australia. For females, one in 10 Aborigines who reach 20 will be dead by 40, compared with one in 50 of the Australian female population. In more than 53 per cent of all deaths of male Aboriginal adults, and 21 per cent of all deaths of female Aboriginal adults, alcohol was mentioned on the death certificate as a significant medical problem. Black self-destruction and violence towards others are intertwined with the most common white man's drug, alcohol.

A Culture of Drinking

Heavy alcohol consumption by Aborigines is not just confined to violent offenders who become drunk just before committing an aggressive act. Most offenders have a long history of alcohol abuse, as do many other people in the community. To say that alcohol is one of the factors that most destroys personal self-esteem and social life in Aboriginal communities is to state the obvious — but it is an obvious fact that requires reiteration and illustration.

Alwyn Peter often described his life as a constant cycle of heavy drinking sessions, bitter gang fighting and self-recrimination after these fights. Alwyn told me when I interviewed him just before his trial that he could drink a 26-ounce bottle of rum in one sitting 'with no trouble handling it'. However, Alwyn's loss of self-control and frequent acts of self-injury and aggression against others demonstrate that 'trouble' inevitably occurred when this limit was reached.

Sometimes Rachel Peter had to call in the manager and the community police to control Alwyn. One researcher, M. Kamien, refers to the effects in rural NSW Aboriginal groups of the necessity for wives to call in the police as a form of external control, a measure which adds further misunderstandings to the relationships between police and Aborigines, as well as adding to domestic disintegration. Yet another observer Beckett says: 'There is irony indeed in a situation where men in their endeavour to defy white damnation, oblige their own wives to betray them to their enemies'.

The beer canteen at Weipa South.

Alwyn said that when he and his friends began a drinking session, 'we only stop drinking when we run out of grog or the canteen closes'. Such sentiments were echoed by many other offenders studied, including a man from Palm Island who bluntly admitted to having a drinking problem, but who continued to drink until he passed out. Social workers' reports referred to accused persons as ones 'with serious drinking problems' or people who 'would drink heavily every night'.

Psychiatrist John Cawte, in attempting to assess Alwyn's level of alcohol consumption, suggested that in a typical drinking session Alwyn might consume six stubbies and half a flagon of port which would total well over 600 grams of alcohol. According to Cawte, 'this is an extraordinarily high amount to drink and to remain conscious at all'.

Given the huge amounts of alcohol consumed by Alwyn Peter and most other offenders, serious doubt should be cast on the popular assumption suggesting that Aborigines cannot hold their liquor. In a very real sense, Aborigines can hold their liquor. They drink so heavily and for so long it is amazing that many can stay on their feet and not collapse. Comparative research is lacking, but personal experience would suggest that whites either slump into unconsciousness or become aggressive at alcohol levels which are lower than those reached by Aborigines before they exhibit similar behaviour. Of relevance here is the fact that black alcoholics have a recovery rate which is far higher than that of whites.

A point does come where Aboriginal drinkers lose control of themselves and mutilate their bodies, hit out at others or slump into a semi-conscious delirium. But the fact that this point is only reached after massive amounts of alcohol should make us change the old adage that, 'Aborigines can't hold their liquor' to 'Aborigines can't hold huge amounts of liquor'.

That drinking on Aboriginal reserves is endemic was abundantly clear from the amounts of alcohol the offenders said they consumed, and from statements made by witnesses and administrators. Don Egan, a former manager at Weipa South, said at least 50 per cent of people at Weipa drank heavily. Egan, in his own private research, attempted to calculate the consumption on Weipa. He carefully noted over a five-day period the amount of alcohol drunk by each person during the hours the canteen was open.

The canteen is open from 5.00 p.m. to 6.00 p.m., closes for an hour between 6.00 and 7.00 p.m., then closes for the night at 10.00 p.m. Egan, a careful and conservative man, calculated that the average amount of beer consumed per person in a four-hour session was two-and-a-half gallons. This is the equivalent of 20 stubbies of beer — a very high average amount in a relatively short time. Queensland flying doctor Howard Stevens has suggested that Egan's figures would probably apply to other Aboriginal reserves as well.

A recent study by social worker Matt Foley supports Egan's and Steven's observations. Foley conducted a survey of the drinking patterns of 83 men who were participating in or had recently attended the Aboriginal and Islander Alcohol Relief Program in Cairns. The program is highly respected by Aboriginal and white social workers. Begun by Rose Colless, it is basically a self-help movement. The program works on principles of self-management, and residents have a significant voice in constructing the centre's rules. Because the residents agreed to co-operate with Foley in the collection of information about drinking behaviour, we can be reasonably sure that his results are accurate.

Rose Colless,
founder of the
Aboriginal and
Islander Alcohol
Rehabilitation
Centre (Douglas
House) in Cairns.

Foley found that although beer (40 per cent), wine (19 per cent) or fortified wine (21.7 per cent) were the most common beverages, 9.6 per cent of residents regularly drank spirits and 7.2 per cent methylated spirits. Just over half of those sampled reported that they drank daily, and one in four of the residents said they would drink more than 10 bottles of beer a day. A further 22.9 per cent reported that they would drink an unspecified amount, but assumed that amount to be over 10 bottles a day.

One-quarter of the men said they drank more than six bottles of wine per day, with a further 20.5 per cent reporting that they drank an unspecified amount of wine. The consumption of spirits was especially disturbing. One in 12 said they would drink more than four bottles of spirits in a day with a further 44.6 per cent reporting an unspecified amount. More often than not, the spirits drunk included methylated spirits.

Most drank at pubs or in parks with relatives or friends. However, one in five drank by themselves. Respondents also said their close family members drank heavily, and nearly two-thirds of the sample believed family members who drank were also having alcohol problems.

One of the major effects of this pattern of heavy drinking was seen in the arrest-rate for public drunkenness of the Aboriginal respondents. In Queensland, it is an offence to be drunk in a public place or on licenced premises, and in contrast to other States, detoxification centres are not widespread. Instead, the problem is defined in criminal terms rather than in social or medical terms, with those arrested often being placed in police watch-houses.

The futility of this approach is demonstrated by the incredibly high number of arrests for drunkenness reported by the residents. One in four reported that they had been arrested for drunkenness 20 times or more, with one in 10 recording more than 50 arrests. Almost all the Aborigines interviewed had been arrested for drunkenness at some time.

On or off reserves, heavy alcohol consumption is widespread and begins at an early age. Alwyn began drinking while still at school and has continued to drink heavily. With friends and relatives also consuming vast amounts of alcohol, it is almost impossible not to drink. Alwyn, as with many others, said drink was always present, and, as people forced him to share in alcohol, he 'could never refuse'.

Most of the fighting on reserves was clearly related to drink, including cases in which criminal charges did not arise. For instance, Alwyn said he only got mad when he was drunk, and then he usually fought with his brother Sidney. In fact, on one occasion a fight developed because Sidney wanted Alwyn to continue drinking with him but Alwyn wanted to go to sleep.

All of Alwyn's relatives confirmed that Alwyn and others at Weipa would get into fights while very drunk. Other self-destructive acts would often follow from drink: property would be destroyed, people would steal from elderly relatives to obtain money to carry on drinking, and occasionally, while in an alcoholic stupor, men and women would stagger around calling out the names of deceased persons.

The link between black drinking and crime is clear, not only from the cases mentioned here, but from published research. Sampson, in his study of fringe dwellers in the Northern Territory, reported that liquor accounted for 89 per cent of all offences for which Aborigines were charged. A more conservative estimate, by the Assistant Commissioner of the Territory's police force, reported that alcohol-related offences might well account for 75 per cent of all Aboriginal crimes. The Australian Institute of Criminology has noted that charges laid against urban Aborigines are generally of a minor nature, but evidence from

South Australia suggests that 60 per cent of these offences (indecent language, disorderly conduct, drunkenness) are alcohol-related. Reported research by Graves and Collett in Port Augusta demonstrates a relationship between receipt of pension cheques and rates of criminal offending by Aborigines.

The results of the massive amount of drinking on Aboriginal communities are disastrous, not only in the level of alcoholism generated but also in contributing towards the Aboriginal rate of petty crime. More important, perhaps, are the effects that alcohol-induced behaviour has on self-esteem and on the social life of the communities. Self-esteem, generally low, is further reduced after heavy drinking and violence. We found violent offenders always displayed guilt and remorse after their crimes, followed by a lowering of self-esteem. The community also suffered from each incident of violence. Elder residents tended to feel ashamed of the publicity attached to each incident and because of kinship between the offender and victim family ties were strained.

Alcohol, perhaps more than any other factor, heightens tribal and family disagreements and jealousies and promotes considerable tensions within Aboriginal communities. The constancies of social life are abandoned because drunken and violent persons offend all the conventions of social interaction. In more traditional communities, drunken people who call out the names of the dead and violate kinship-avoidance rules add further to the tension and insecurity felt by the group.

The House of Representatives Standing Committee in their report, *Alcohol Problems of Aborigines*, pointed out that heavy drinking has led to a breakdown of traditional society. They found that the authority of clan elders was eroded as a result of their lack of experience with alcohol and that social control mechanisms were not available in the community to deal with alcohol abuse. Alcohol stopped Aborigines from dealing with their individual destinies and that of their communities. It directly contributed to the sense of powerlessness endemic in many Aboriginal societies.

Multiple Causes, Multiple Solutions

According to the House of Representatives Standing Committee on Aboriginal Affairs, 90 per cent of men and 80 per cent of women on some Queensland reserves drink heavily. In seeking reasons for this, we should begin by looking at what people in these communities say about their own and other people's drinking.

Let us start with Alwyn Peter, who said he drank when he was sad and lonely. At Mapoon, where alcohol was not available, Alwyn said he did not feel the need to drink because he was happy while hunting, fishing and feeling close to his relatives. Alwyn's brother Douglas, on the other hand, said he was sure people drank just because alcohol was present at Weipa South. But Douglas is only partly correct because on reserves where alcohol is not allowed, flourishing 'sly grog' rackets abound.

Alwyn's grandmother, Maggie Don, said she believed that people drank because they were unhappy and, as with Alwyn, pointed out that there is no need to drink at Mapoon 'because people feel better'. Most of the offenders mentioned in this book gave explanations for their heavy drinking that suggested they drank because they were sad and lonely. Some offenders also reported that they started to drink after leaving school because of the boredom and lack of work available on the reserves, although others saw drink also as 'a way to become a man'. Many pointed out the difficulties of refusing alcohol in social situations in which everyone else consumes and that it is considered 'deviant' not to participate in heavy drinking sessions.

While these explanations may lack the jargon and empiricism of the social scientists, they offer clearer insights into drinking. For the meanings that people give to their actions — in this case their drinking behaviour — are always important in understanding a social problem. In the words they choose to describe the reasons they drink, clues to the causes of excessive consumption are revealed.

These factors can be classified into three groups. Firstly, we have those psychological and social reasons that create a culture of drinking. Secondly, environmental factors are present in the communities from which the drinkers come. Thirdly, historical and cultural factors have made alcohol a substitute for more traditional ways of relating to others.

Let us begin with the psychological and social factor. Virtually every commission of inquiry into Aboriginal alcoholism has pointed to the lack of autonomy, pride and self-esteem existing among native people. After generations of white domination, Aboriginal people have created their own culture — what one writer has called an 'alcohol culture' — in order to obtain a measure of self-respect.

The characteristics of this culture, seen on Queensland reserves, include drinking large quantities of beer or wine, brawling to establish manliness, staggering around to accentuate the effects of alcohol and glorying in past accounts of drunken exploits and fights. Despite being fully aware of the consequences of drinking — police reprisals, personal injury, family and community violence and lack of money to buy other commodities — most of the individuals mentioned in this book saw drinking as a way of 'feeling better' and 'getting on top of things'. They saw drinking as an occasion for sharing conviviality and seeking esteem.

The alcohol culture promotes drinking and fighting as positive virtues and as giving Aboriginal life a distinctive quality, one which emphasises the present and not the future. Beckett's observations confirm this point. He says 'the things on which Aborigines now place most value are the immediate things of the present. This is due to the collapse of a tradition in which the future took care of itself by being continuous with the past'.

In nearly all the cases described so far, it is apparent that offenders, in their youth, aspired to be part of the alcohol culture. On most Queensland reserves, children as young as seven play games in which they imitate some of the older men in their singing and dancing behaviour, often also emulating their staggering gait. Alwyn recounts how he begged for a drink when liquor was brought home, and as a teenager bragged about getting drunk. As others have noted, 'the first episode of drunkenness was akin to an initiation ceremony'. Once Alwyn and his friends became financially independent after leaving school, they drank regularly and heavily, perpetuating the behaviour of their elders.

In such a culture it is almost impossible not to drink. For how else is one to achieve self-esteem and achieve, even temporarily, some inner peace? Psychiatrist Harry Eastwell, when giving evidence on Alwyn's behalf, said: 'I don't think there was much reason why Alwyn should not have drunk . . . he and others didn't have many sources of self-esteem to, as it were, hang their hats on . . . alcohol can raise a set of better feelings about yourself and you are at ease with yourself for a while'.

Those who do not become part of the alcohol culture are often referred to as 'missionaries', as individuals who are strange and queer. Sampson, in *The Camp at Wallaby Cross*, observed that in a grogging community the moral onus is reversed and it is the abstainer who must apologise. 'Because they are deviant',

Sampson writes, 'temperate men in grogging communities are put on the defensive'. Indeed, at Yarrabah, some Aborigines who return to the reserve after drying out in a detoxification centre tell of their peers physically forcing them to resume drinking. I have talked to young Aborigines from Yarrabah who were beaten up because they refused to join a grogging party.

Peer-group pressure, although a significant element in general Australian drinking patterns, is of particular importance for Aborigines. When for example, alcohol is offered to a young man by an older man with traditional responsibility to teach or assist him, rejection by the young man is seen as a rejection of the relationship. In traditionally oriented Aboriginal groups, kinship pressure makes it impossible for an individual to drink moderately or to abstain. Only if the kin group abstains is this possible. Downing, referring to the Northern Territory, observes that 'the tribally oriented people are either heavy drinkers or teetotallers — there is no inbetween. . . one must belong to an abstaining group . . . if they are with a drinking group, they drink'.

The search for self-esteem through the alcohol culture is closely interlocked with the second major set of factors in Aboriginal drinking: these are related to the social and economic conditions on reserves and communities. Factors of this sort, discussed elsewhere in this book, relate to employment, health, nutrition, housing, and lack of education opportunities and specific vocational skills. By any standards, Aborigines are poor, and poverty worsens alcohol problems. The stress involved in over-crowded housing; the discomfort of ill health; the cycle of meaningless employment followed by unemployment; the constant boredom and irrelevance of most educational pursuits — all these make alcohol and the alcohol culture a convenient escape mechanism.

Psycho-social and environmental factors strongly influence the patterns of heavy drinking that have been observed. Psycho-social factors appear to be more relevant to tribal and reserve communities; environmental factors appear to be most significant in metropolitan areas and some country towns. However, both sets of factors are heavily inter-related, and both are intertwined with the historical and cultural context of Aboriginal–white contact.

The seeds of the alcohol culture were sown when Aborigines were forced to submit to white domination. Communities of Aborigines grew up on the fringes of country towns and pastoral stations all over Australia; for many, this was the only practical alternative to starvation or violent death. In the process, every element of traditional Aboriginal life, religious, social, economic and physical, was severely threatened.

European goods such as steel axes and knives, already eagerly sought by Aboriginal tribes, replaced traditional instruments. Western food, tobacco and alcohol also exerted a tremendous influence on the pattern of migration of Aborigines to white society. Stanner observed that 'The stimulants . . . precipitated the exodus. Individuals, families and parties of friends simply went away to places where the avidly desired things could be obtained.'

So, dispossessed of land and tradition, starved of nutrition and pride, diseased and abused by whites, according to Aboriginal elder, Grandfather Koori, they 'lost the law and lost themselves. Then they welcomed the white man who brought them the grog and tobacco and flour. They cringed to him like whipped dogs cringe to the man who kicks and feeds them. And (they) lost all value, started spending their lives looking for grog and waiting to die'.

As in other examples of colonial exploitation of native peoples, liquor for the Aborigines assumed a special and heightened significance. Its exhilarating effects provided a novel diversion when traditional ways of life were discredited or impracticable. When reserves were formed, liquor was prohibited and punishments were severe, but the attraction it exerted for the Aborigines was too strongly ingrained to be impaired by mere legal sanctions.

Prohibitions did not stop Aborigines drinking; rather, it changed the pattern of drinking and heightened its significance. Spirits and cheap fortified wines were preferred because they were easier to conceal; bootlegging and moonshining were rife; methylated spirits and other alcohol substances available from stores were consumed; liquor was drunk quickly so police could not confiscate it. The characteristics of the alcohol culture, now a familiar part of the lives of Alwyn Peter, Oscar, Harold and all the others, were accentuated and stylised during the prohibition period.

Over time, the drinking habits of residents on reserves and fringe communities began to take on a life of their own. Collman's research indicates that the consumption and sharing of liquor is a method which Aborigines use to construct their relationships with each other and to build up credit. This means that men spend any surplus income they earn on liquor for their friends and kin in order to maintain their right to credit. In group drinking, in sharing one's grog, Aboriginal people attempt to develop funds of credit against long-term uncertainties by spending current surpluses on liquor.

Violence frequently erupts in these groups. Many of our dossiers revealed that men were bodily thrown out of drinking groups because their credit had run out. Sometimes, men would bash or stab their wives because pension cheques were spent entirely on food, leaving no money available for drink. To the Aboriginal male, the social ostracism that follows from not being able to join a drinking group is often severe.

The alcohol culture has arisen for a number of reasons and performs a number of social functions. Not only does it serve as a psychological escape device from debilitating social and economic conditions but it also, temporarily at least, raises self-esteem and a sense of feeling 'good' about the world. Alcohol has become the focal point for social occasions, as well as a means of payment of debt to kin and friends. It makes some Aborigines feel, in the words of one reserve dweller, 'just like a white man' — strong, powerful, in control and indestructible.

Another use of alcohol in Aboriginal communities is worth noting. Anthropologist John Taylor has reported that at Edward River, people occasionally use alcohol to solve disputes. The disputes or 'wrongs' are already present before heavy drinking. By consuming large quantities of alcohol and becoming intoxicated, people who have been aggrieved in the past can hit or abuse others who have offended them. Being drunk, they are free from responsibility for their actions and can obtain vindication with fewer personal or community repercussions.

Aboriginal drinking behaviour is, therefore, not merely haphazard or confused mass intoxication, but an activity conducted to specific social patterns. Basically it is open, public, binge drinking, what Noonan has called 'shared social activity aimed at ritual oblivion with little differentiation in the drinking patterns between sexes'.

Recent white man's drugs that have permeated Aboriginal communities serve the same functions. Fuel and glue sniffing, for example, occur in town and reserve areas among young boys and girls and are indications not only of the stress factors in adolescence but also of the aimlessness and culture-conflict felt by youthful Aborigines. The instant feelings of exhilaration, comradeship and well-being experienced by glue and petrol inhalers have their counterparts in adult Aboriginal drinking groups. Although, from reports, violence among youth who use these substances is not as savage and deadly as that which results from heavy alcohol consumption, fights and vendettas often arise as personal controls loosen.

With multiple causes to the heavy drinking patterns observed among Aborigines it would be foolish to search for simple one-dimensional solutions. Unfortunately some politicians do just this. Des Frawley, the National Party Member for Caboolture in Queensland, recently suggested that alcohol should be banned for all Aborigines. Frawley's contention that Aborigines 'cannot hold their grog' is hardly supported by the evidence available from this study and besides, imposed prohibition just does not work. Indeed, as with prohibition in the United States, ways are always found to obtain alcohol. Historically, prohibition for Aborigines accentuated the alcohol culture.

The prohibition of alcohol to most Aborigines until 1967 did little to reduce consumption of liquor. It merely ensured that drinking did not occur in public places, made Aborigines dependent on whites for supplies and hence vulnerable to economic and sexual exploitation.

Self-imposed prohibition may well be a different matter. Some Queensland reserve councils, such as Doomadgee's, have not taken up the option given by the Queensland Government in 1971, allowing canteens if Aboriginal councils so desire. Some outstation movements, such as at Aurukun, have banned alcohol. This measure has proved partly successful, although flying doctor Howard Stevens has noted that at Aurukun, as at Laura and Coen, alcohol consumption is related to patterns of work. Stevens has observed that when the men are not working and are in town all the time, they are constantly drunk and fight with each other. On the other hand, when they are out mustering for some months they come back looking fit and more contented.

Alcohol clinics run by Aborigines appear to have some success. Douglas House in Cairns, which runs a drying-out centre as well as a farm at Daintree, organises itself along therapeutic community lines. Aborigines control the centres, vote democratically on how the centre and farm should be run, and stress Aboriginal ways of community life and counselling. Training courses for Aboriginal welfare workers from nearby communities and reserves assist re-integration into these areas and serve to educate the communities on the dangers of excessive consumption. Attempts are made to use traditional features of Aboriginal life such as dance and painting during this educative process. Proper evaluation studies of these methods are lacking, but preliminary observation would suggest that they offer much more than white-controlled, medically oriented institutional programs.

Solutions to the vicious cycle linking alcohol and violence do not ultimately lie with specific education or alcohol prevention programs. They will be found in a more comprehensive approach which brings back to Aboriginal people a sense of self-worth and community esteem. As with health, housing, nutrition and education, this esteem will only be forthcoming when Aborigines determine their own future and escape the paternalism that has characterised white government and bureaucratic policies for so long. Until this occurs, alcoholism and violence, with prisons, juvenile homes and high death-rates, will continue to plague Aboriginal communities.

6 Killing Me Quietly

The Spectre of Imprisonment

When Alwyn, Oscar or Duncan strangle, stab or bash others, their actions are direct, observable and easily recognisable forms of aggression, as is the violence against the Kalkadoons by white pastoralists, or the shooting of Aborigines by colonists at Mapoon.

But violence comes in several degrees and is delivered in a number of ways. For example, it would seem reasonable to call the actions of the police and government officials at Mapoon, violent — enforced transportation from one's land and the burning of one's home are recognised by those affected as violence.

Other actions are generally not recognised by the community as violent. Air and water pollution, defective cars and asbestos poisoning tend to be redefined as 'accidents' or 'unfortunate but necessary practices'. The results of these practices, however, lead to death, serious injury and trauma just as more direct aggression does.

Similarly, it can be argued that the imprisonment of Aborigines for offences which would not lead to incarceration if committed by whites and a government's neglect of basic health on Aboriginal reserves are aggressive or violent acts that are as damaging in their consequences as more overt actions. It is, therefore, reasonable to call them violent actions even if we are using the word in a more general way than usual.

Let us turn first to the issue of imprisonment. Although specific information is lacking, available material suggests that Aborigines may have the world's highest imprisonment rate. In 1981, the Director of the Australian Institute of Criminology, William Clifford, estimated that between 500 and 1000 Aborigines per 100,000 were in jail throughout the country, whereas the imprisonment rate for Australia generally was 67 per 100,000.

Clifford pointed out that Aborigines represented only one per cent of the Australian population but 30 per cent of the number in prison. From statistics available, proportionately more Aborigines have a record of repeated imprisonment: one third of Aboriginal prisoners had received three or more previous prison sentences, compared with 23 per cent of non-Aboriginal prisoners.

These imprisonment rates for Aborigines are far greater than any others we could obtain from within or outside Australia. For example, incarceration rates for Fiji are 218.1 per 100,000; for New Zealand 109.3; for Holland 20.0 per 100,000. When the Aboriginal figures are compared with imprisonment rates for migrant groups the same discrepancies emerge. Italians have a low rate of 39.79; Greeks 39.15; Maltese, a group with a higher than average figure for migrants, have a rate of 75.83.

In Queensland, it is extremely difficult to obtain separate statistics on Aboriginal imprisonment rates because the State Government considers that the keeping of such statistics is essentially 'racist'. In a magnificent piece of logic, the Queensland Minister for Welfare Services said that the State did not keep statistical records of the race of prisoners. For, according to the Minister, 'if a government starts a policy like that it will end up with statistics based on religious and political beliefs'. Such views are not shared by the Australian Bureau of Statistics, and we know from census figures presented in the Senate in 1981 that Aboriginal and Islander children make up 11.9 per cent of juveniles in Queensland care institutions, although making up only two per cent of the State's population. However, these figures include homes for the physically and mentally handicapped, as well as homes for delinquents, so they must be treated cautiously.

Nevertheless, in a survey of Aborigines and Torres Strait Islanders in Queensland prisons, social worker Merrilyn Walton calculated that males in these groups are taken into custody at least seven times more frequently than would be predicted from their proportion of the total population. For females the figures are considerably higher. The female Aboriginal and Islander population is 20,727 — about 1.92 per cent of the total female population — but they represent nearly 30 per cent of the prison population. Walton found that almost half of all Aboriginal people in prison said that they had other immediate family members who had also been sentenced to a term in jail. As

The old lock up at Weipa South.

discussed in Chapter 1, almost 80 per cent of the homicide and
serious assault offenders on Queensland Aboriginal reserves and
communities had previous convictions.

Alwyn Peter had a string of convictions, some of which had
landed him in jail. In 1973 he was convicted of obscene language
and in 1975 and 1976, of unlawfully using cars. Two further convictions followed, one for stealing and the other for not paying a
fine in connection with a previous car-stealing charge. The latter
offence led to six months imprisonment. Three years later, at the
beginning of 1979, Alwyn was charged again with stealing and
unlawful use of a car. Towards the end of that year, he was
charged with receiving stolen goods, and for another unlawful use
of a motor vehicle. In the middle of that year, Alwyn was also
convicted of discharging a firearm in a public place.

As Walton's figures suggest, often several members of an
immediate family are imprisoned. Alwyn's brother Sidney spent
six months at the Westbrooke training centre for juveniles for
smashing the office windows of the Department of Aboriginal
and Islander Advancement at Weipa South. Later, he was sent to
Stuart Prison, Townsville, for seriously assaulting his lover,
Geraldine.

Among the possible reasons for the enormously high rate of

imprisonment among Aboriginal people are at least four which relate both to the criminal justice system and to the social and cultural position Aborigines find themselves in. Let us turn to the first of these four explanations: the possibility that Aboriginal people are more criminal in nature than other groups in Australia.

The difficulty that arises when attempts are made to answer this question comes from teasing out the rate of crimes committed by Aborigines from the biases inherent in our criminal justice system. But if convictions are any guide to criminality — a debatable proposition — there can be no doubt that the Aboriginal crime rate is extremely high.

The homicide and serious assault figures for people on reserves and communities in Queensland would indicate that the rate is 10 times higher than for whites. But these comparisons do not include Aborigines in urban areas and therefore are local figures only. However, crime figures from all over Australia show similar patterns and we therefore have to conclude that the actual rate of crime is far greater among native Australians than any other ethnic or social group in the country. Most of these convictions are for minor offences such as drunkenness, obscence language and disorderly behaviour, but recent studies indicate a definite movement from minor offences to major ones such as aggravated assault, breaking and entering, and stealing.

The extraordinarily high Aboriginal crime figures result from obvious biases in the criminal justice system. Many years ago, Elizabeth Eggleston's research demonstrated that in comparison with whites, blacks tend to be arrested rather than summonsed; to have multiple rather than single charges laid; to have less chance of being granted bail; and to spend a longer time in custody before their court appearance. Studies done more recently in New South Wales by the State Bureau of Crime Research and Statistics have confirmed Eggleston's research.

All these studies demonstrate that the police, having very wide powers of arrest for minor offences, are much more likely to arrest an Aborigine than a white person. The research also suggests that for these same offences, the judiciary are more likely to fine a white person for crimes for which many Aborigines would be imprisoned.

Research comparing police and judicial practices with major white and black offenders are singularly lacking, but it is possible that the opposite result prevails. For example, the research reported in this book indicates that most offences leading to death on reserves result in a charge of manslaughter, rather than murder, and that sentences given are lenient. It is possible that if the victims were white rather than black, no such leniency would prevail.

The anecdotal evidence of racism and discrimination among criminal justice personnel strongly suggests that Aborigines are discriminated against in that system. In Queensland, the Government's *Report of the Committee of Inquiry into the Enforcement of Criminal Law in Queensland* found ample evidence of such discrimination. The report said, 'in the case of Aborigines, there were sad stories ranging from allegations of misunderstanding down to frank brutality'.

In illustrating this point, the Committee reported a taped conversation, later introduced in court, between a police inspector, a uniformed sergeant of police and a civilian. The inspector was aware the conversation was being taped; the others were not.

Sgt	The old blacks are still playing up?
Insp.	The blacks.
Sgt	Hey?
Insp.	Yea, um, yeah.
Sgt	Want a bloody, good waddy over their nut.
Insp.	Orh, they have done the wrong thing by those people you know.
Sgt	What?
Insp.	They've done the wrong thing by those people.
Sgt	What by the blacks?
Insp.	Yeah.
Civ.	Ha, ha, ha.
Sgt	Didn't kill enough of the buggers.

The conversation continues in a similar vein until terminated by the sergeant's suggesting that 'the good old days are gone with the blacks. You can't give them a bloody razzle-dazzle like you used to be able to'.

It is this very 'razzle dazzle' which is the subject of many complaints among Queensland Aborigines. Occasionally, examples of a more subtle form of 'razzle dazzle' emerge. In Queensland, two years ago, police charged a woman with vagrancy because she lived with an Aborigine. The woman's defence counsel pointed out that this law had been repealed several years before and the police prosecutor withdrew the charge; but the fact that the charge was even brought to court points strongly to police harrassment.

A third explanation for the high rate of Aboriginal crime could be that Aborigines have social problems which bring them directly into conflict with the law. There can be no doubt that problems such as drunkenness, high unemployment rates and cultural conflict worsen police-black contacts, as can be seen in the case of public drinking.

Despite the arguments suggesting that whites drink just as much as blacks, there is abundant evidence to suggest that Aborigines have a major alcoholism problem, possibly unparalleled in industrialised countries. Moreover, much Aboriginal drinking is public, on the streets and in parks, and so more likely to attract police attention. Similar conflicts arise from high rates of Aboriginal unemployment, homelessness and geographical mobility. The part that white Australians have taken in creating cultural conflict, and in the introduction of alcohol, is discussed elsewhere in this book.

Fourthly, high crime and imprisonment rates could arise from the conflict between Aboriginal customs and white law. The two systems are separately administered. In Queensland, for example, there are no Aboriginal judges, magistrates, lawyers, probation officers or child care officers, and only two black State policemen. In remote areas of the state, Aborigines are still being tried and sentenced by untrained local Justices of the Peace, usually businessmen of long standing, whose ignorance of the law is often matched only by their determination to uphold the 'community standards' of local whites. Even in the best courts, however, Aborigines get a rough deal. Outside reserves, in which Aborigines deal with minor offenders, the refusal of Australian jurisdictions to ensure fair representation of various racial groups on juries guarantees bias. An unemployed black reserve dweller from Doomadgee, or a fringe dweller from Mt Isa, does not receive 'trial by their peers' when they stand before a jury of staunch white citizens whose knowledge of Aborigines comes from racist textbooks and observation of drunks in the street.

Numerous recommendations have been made by the Law Reform Commission and the *Report on Law and Poverty in Australia*, headed by Professor Ron Sackville, but no substantial measures have been taken in Queensland to bridge the cultural gaps between white law and Aboriginal culture.

Training given to police on Aboriginal matters is limited and cursory. Similarly, magistrates are woefully ignorant of the problems and difficulties Aborigines face when questioned by police: the tendency of blacks to say 'yes' to every question; their inability to understand legal terms; their different conceptions of such factors as time and age — all are rarely considered by lower court adjudicators.

Throughout the dossiers, many examples came to our attention of interrogation techniques which illustrated police insensitivity to Aboriginal linguistic problems during interviews of suspects. There was often the tendency for an accused person to agree with a policeman during a preliminary interview, but to deny the implication of his agreement at a later stage. Two examples, used by the Public Defender when checking with his clients the accuracy of the initial police interrogation, illustrate this point:

I only agreed with the detective here because I thought that was what he wanted me to say.

I really can't remember hitting her with the woomera. I do know that the woomera had blood on it but I think she might have got this from the cut under her arm. I only said (I hit her) because I gathered that he wanted me to say that I hit her with it. I can't actually remember hitting her with it.

Other measures which would help to alleviate the cultural problems Aborigines face are yet to be introduced in Queensland. Vagrancy and drunkenness offences are not yet abolished; fines are still 'fixed' rather than being related to an offender's income; a bail system still operates which depends on a person's ability to buy his freedom; arrest, rather than the use of a summons, predominates in many areas. No guaranteed interpreters are provided for people with little English, nor guaranteed representation for Aborigines interrogated by the police. Much remains to be done.

A related but much more vexed question has been considered by the Australian Law Reform Commission. The Commission considered the extent to which customary law should be recognised and applied by existing courts and the extent to which Aboriginal communities should be empowered to enforce their own laws.

They correctly recognised two pressures of relevance to both these questions. The first relates to the impact that contact with whites has had on Aboriginal culture. They noted that such contact has so affected the lives of many Aborigines that Aboriginal customary law now has little, if any, significance. On the other hand, the second pressure, that of land rights, is a reflection of the desires of other Aborigines to seek to return to more traditional ways.

In traditional society, certain acts, both of commission and omission, constitute serious offences. These acts include: sacrilege; unauthorised sorcery; incest; cohabitation with certain kin; abduction or enticement of women; adultery with certain kin; physical neglect of certain relatives; unauthorised physical assault.

In serious offences such as adultery, elopement or even physical injury, spearing was often the penalty but was not generally intended to kill the offender. Probably no more than five per cent of all Aboriginal communities could now be classified as having maintained their traditional ways sufficiently to warrant the retention of these offences and this traditional punishment.

On Queensland reserves, traditional practices and laws have broken down considerably. Alwyn Peter's reserve of Weipa South, for example, has been so distorted by stifling white control and intertribal mixing that few traditional features remain. However, when studying the dossiers, I noted both the amount of adultery that occurred and the degree to which an aggrieved person considered this a serious breach of his or her rights. In one sense, it could be argued that when Alwyn killed Deidre he was punishing her for being unfaithful to him.

On the other hand, it is difficult to sustain the motive of jealousy as a justification for the men and women who killed their unfaithful lovers. On Queensland reserves, there is probably not one Aborigine who does not appreciate that to kill or assault another person is a serious offence leading inexorably to police action. Alwyn's remorse and guilt over his crime also suggests that his offence occurred not out of traditional desires to punish her for her adultery but rather from a drunken, jealous moment of spontaneous anger. Certainly no sympathy towards Alwyn was extended by the community at Weipa.

Similarly, it can be argued that episodes of rage and anger such as those displayed by Alwyn and other offenders are like losses of temper shown in traditional times. However, as anthropologist John Taylor points out, there is a significant difference between contemporary violent anger and that displayed in former times. Alcohol exaggerates real or imagined wrongs and diminishes the ability of people to control their actions. Because of this, reserve dwellers accept the fact that individuals who drink are lacking in responsibility and self-control. Consequently, it is not uncommon to discover people taking control of drunks or hiding potential weapons. Maggie Don, for example, hid the knife given to her by Deidre on the night of her murder.

Alcohol, real or imagined wrongs, together with a distorted cultural pattern causing individuals to seek redress for these wrongs in a violent fashion have, says Taylor, 'provided a devastating mix in present-day Aboriginal communities'. This 'devasting mix' is the result of the white invasion and subsequent political insensitivity to Aboriginal problems.

The Australian Law Reform Commission has tried valiantly to grapple with these problems (their specific recommendations are discussed in Chapter 9), but still Aboriginal people both as offenders and victims, suffer the consequences. Some offenders suffer more than one punishment. Imprisonment is often followed by community ostracism, or at times a 'payback' beating occurs. Both victim and offender suffer because traditional law has broken down, only to be superimposed by a law that is foreign to both. So, for many Aborigines caught between the old and new ways, justice appears to have been forgotten.

The Other Side of Death

Not only are Aborigines imprisoned at a rate far exceeding any other group in the nation but they are also dying more frequently and at an earlier age than other Australians. As part of the research for this book, I was able to obtain, for the first time, mortality rates for Queensland reserves.

With medical sociologist Jake Najman and researcher Robyn Lincoln, every death on Aboriginal reserves between 1976 and 1980 was analysed and standardised by age and sex to allow for comparisons with the Queensland population. Four basic causes of death were located: accident or violence; infections; cardiovascular causes; other causes such as cancer and prematurity.

Under the first category were included not only deaths by violent attack such as stab wound in fights or drunken brawls but also drownings, suicides and motor vehicle accidents. Our age-and sex-standardised figures, compared with the Queensland population, are startling. The Aboriginal death rate is 2.33 times the Queensland rate (average per year: Aborigines 16.04 per 10,000; Queensland 6.88). When reserves which received people from other tribes and which were close to urban centres were compared with reserves which were non-receivers and relatively far away from urban areas, even more obvious differences emerged. The former category of reserves (Yarrabah, Weipa, Palm, Hopevale and Cherbourg) had a death rate of 25.06 per

10,000 compared with 9.14 per 10,000 for the other communities. These results confirm what has been shown in previous Chapters. Violence in all forms is endemic in Queensland Aboriginal communities. Considering that these figures contain deaths by motor vehicles as well as deaths by violence, the comparisons with Queensland as a whole are even more clear-out. Whites own more cars proportionally than Aborigines, and as the white rate for motor vehicle accidents is high, the difference between the two sets of figures is increased. Yet even with the most conservative estimate, Aborigines are 2.33 times more likely than whites to die violently.

More dramatic figures than these were found when deaths caused by infections were analysed. The Aboriginal reserve figure here is 38.3 per 10,000; the Queensland figure is a mere 0.43. In other words, the Aboriginal rate is 89 times that of the State. As with violent deaths, differences between 'receiver/urban reserves' and 'non-receiver/isolated communities', exist, although they are not as large as for other causes of death (36.46 per receivers and 40.64 for non-receivers).

Deaths in this category arise from infections such as gastro-enteritis, septicaemia, pneumonia, viral infections and influenza. We found that deaths from gastroenteritis, for example, occurred not only among small children and babies but also among men and women of all ages. Nowhere could we find evidence to demonstrate that tribal Aborigines suffered gastro-enteritis at anywhere near the rates we found on reserves. The only possible conclusion was that the general conditions of hygiene on reserves were responsible for the high rate of infectious diseases and deaths.

When I have looked at the physical conditions on reserves, I have always been struck by the lack of adequate water and sewerage facilities, an observation that has been confirmed by other researchers. Writer Sylvia Monk, in researching her new book on Queensland Aboriginal communities, reports that it was not until 1979 that the first water tap was installed at an Aboriginal shanty town outside Townsville. Lack of these and other basic facilities are apparent on many other communities and often lead to outbreaks of infectious diseases.

In 1979 at Palm Island, for example, 153 Aborigines were hospitalised with an undiagnosed illness. Symptoms of the illness included diarrhoea, vomiting attacks, loss of balance and complete disorientation. The illness was initially caused, according to Charles Porter, the Queensland Minister for Aboriginal

Affairs, by 'people eating too many green mangoes'. Scepticism about this explanation was expressed by many doctors and politicians, including Aboriginal Senator, Neville Bonner, who asked for the Minister's dismissal. Bonner rightly pointed out that if a similar outbreak had occurred in Brisbane 'there would be considerable panic'. Although no one was sure what factors had triggered the outbreak, microbiologists thought that contaminated water was responsible. As people on the island had for months boiled water before drinking it because of its foul taste and colour, it is not surprising that the outbreak happened. Chris George of the Aboriginal and Islanders' Medical Centre summed it up well when she said, 'Townsville people wouldn't put up with stinking water that they had to boil before use'.

Great difficulty arises when attempts are made to isolate the factors responsible for the third category, cardio-vascular related deaths, which are characteristic of all Aboriginal reserve deaths. The medical literature would suggest that such deaths are related to stress, so we suspect that general problems of frustration caused by overall living conditions on reserves contribute towards the rate. Alcohol and cigarette consumption on reserves seems to be extraordinarily high, and consumption of these drugs is generally associated with tension and insecurity. But much more research needs to be done; these explanations of the cause of death have to be treated cautiously.

Regardless of the causes of cardio-vascular deaths, the figures speak for themselves. The total rate for cardio-vascular deaths on Aboriginal reserves is 80.9 per 10,000 which is twice the overall Queensland rate of 39.09. As with other forms of death, differences exist between those reserves which are 'receivers' and close to urban settlements, and those which are 'non-receivers' and more isolated. The former group have a mortality rate of 90.46 per 10,000; in the latter group, the figure is less than half: 41.14.

The fourth cause of death studied is a category that includes cancer, prematurity, diabetes and deaths caused by alcohol poisoning and alcoholic asphyxiation such as choking on one's own vomit. The same depressing contrasts recur between Aborigines and the whole of Queensland. For the reserves the mortality rate is 65.42; the figure for the State is 30.88. There are no differences between different groups of reserves.

So far, we have only mentioned those factors that lead to death, but many other health problems remain. Syphilis is widespread; if Queensland parallels the Northern Territory, there is possibly a

20 times higher incidence of the disease among blacks than whites. The eye disease, trachoma, is also widespread in Queensland communities despite prevention programs.

Clues to the reasons behind the abnormally high death and illness rates among Aborigines can be found in the work of the National Trachoma and Health Program run by Professor Fred Hollows. According to Hollows, the diseases he has observed among Aboriginal communities while working on the Trachoma Program were very firmly rooted in the appalling living conditions on the communities. A doctor might be able to ameliorate, even temporarily cure, some of the diseases found, but Hollows believes that they will continue until living conditions are improved.

Such conclusions have been reached by other medical observers. Flying doctor Howard Stevens, in evidence to Mr Justice Dunn in the Alwyn Peter case, said that all he was doing was treating symptoms and not causes. Unfortunately, when Stevens attempted to describe the social conditions on reserves related to the illnesses he treated, the Crown Prosecutor challenged the relevance of his testimony and his qualifications to talk on non-medical matters. Mr Justice Dunn agreed with the Prosecutor and Stevens' testimony was summarily terminated.

However, in a report to the Queensland Director-General of Health, 14 doctors, including Stevens, said the standard of Aboriginal health is 'by far the lowest in the Australian community and would not be tolerated by those sectors of the community if in a similar situation'. The doctors in their survey of conditions found that one-third of Queensland Aboriginal families surveyed were homeless, and that 63 per cent of the houses were rated by interviewers as being of a very poor standard. Further, 97 per cent of houses available in Aboriginal communities were badly overcrowded.

All these factors contributed, the report said, to the high mortality and illness figures. These figures were compounded as well by the fact that less than half the respondents had ever visited a dentist, and 64 per cent could not afford medicine. Despite the seriousness of the report's findings, the doctors had received no reply from either the Director-General or the State or federal governments 18 months after the findings were submitted.

A lack of response from the Queensland Government was hardly surprising. The report, in its main recommendation, called for the Queensland Department of Aboriginal and Islander

Advancement to withdraw from Aboriginal reserves as a first step in improving the standard of Aboriginal health in Queensland. Similar calls have been made by other individuals and organisations, all of whom harshly criticise governments for not allowing Aborigines to run their own health services. The National Director of Community Aid Abroad, Harry Martin has expressed such a view. According to Martin, 'international aid agencies can shame the governments by providing Aboriginal people with money to get on with these desperately needed programs'.

Similarly, Professor Hollows is adamant that 'nothing significant will be achieved until Aborigines control their own service and tailor it to their needs and culture'. He admits that, during the Trachoma Program, 'most of the mistakes that were made went against the advice of our Aboriginal advisors'. Even the most recent government report on Aboriginal health reached the same conclusion. The report, by an inter-departmental committee of government departments, recommended that further federal funding be directed away from State programs to those in which Aborigines had substantial control. As the report said, most of the $280 million a year spent on Aboriginal health goes to the States to pay for white trained staff and capital equipment, and very few Aborigines are employed at policy or administrative levels.

The World Council of Churches Report in 1981 sums it all up. The observers from the Council found 'children with nose and ear infections, numerous people with eye diseases or even blindness and many suffering from malnutrition'. They also, perceptively, saw the environmental conditions which caused these problems:

> Inadequate or no housing, poor water supply, lack of sanitation facilities, displacement from traditional lands, unemployment and a sense of rejection often leading to alcoholism were all too common conditions.

All these factors were present in the Peter family. In common with thousands of other Aboriginal families in Queensland, the Peters had medical histories that would be utterly foreign to 99 per cent of white Australians. Seven of Maggie Don's 11 children died during childhood. Rachel, Alwyn's mother, had several hospital admissions for chest pains caused by infections and still other admissions for eye problems and cranial nerve palsy. Her medical history also showed 'routine presentations' for chest infections, mild trauma, urinary tract infections and replenishment of drugs for hypertension. Alwyn's father Simon had a similar history.

Alwyn had hospital admissions on several occasions for infected ears, scabies, severe attacks of asthma and upper respiratory tract infections. Indeed, throughout his adolescence, he was troubled by a constant ringing in his ears caused by infections, and contracted pneumonia several times. He was also admitted for car accidents and self-inflicted injuries. When asked to comment on the influence of Alwyn's mother's many illnesses on her children, a Weipa Hospital doctor would only say 'the family situation seems very disruptive'. No one could disagree with this masterly understatement.

The Consequences

The high rate of imprisonment and the prevalence of death and illness on reserves lead to both obvious and subtle consequences. With mortality and imprisonment rates among the highest in the world — perhaps the highest — Aboriginal communities are continually fragmented.

Children lose their mothers and fathers at an early age; parents suffer the heartbreak of seeing their children die very young. Before they die, all sections of the community — women, men and young people — often suffer the indignity of white criminal justice. Police interrogation, the humiliation of court and finally the squalor of prison become hallmarks of growing up black in Queensland.

Most directly affected are Aboriginal males. It is the men who mainly die of violence, alcohol-related illnesses, cardio-vascular conditions and of other ailments. It is they who end up in juvenile institutions and finally in jails. With their traditional authority eroded by severe social change and their numbers depleted by crime and illness, Aboriginal men often present a moving picture to their womenfolk and to their children. As a result, some Aboriginal families are becoming matrifocal, with women being expected to take the initiative not only in child-rearing, but also in organising the household, finances, disciplining children, negotiating with white authority and in planning the future.

However, that future is uncertain, for death is an everyday occurrence on Aboriginal reserves. Without adequate financial resources to improve their lot and without control of their own land, Aborigines live more for the present than for the future.

Patterns of imprisonment tend to be repeated. Many juveniles offend continually; by the time they are in their mid-twenties, they have very serious records of conviction, and have spent a large part of their adult lives in jails. The result is that they have no stable marriage or family relationships, and are likely to offend again and go back to prison.

Despite the pain of imprisonment, this often becomes the only life they know. When conducting research for this book, my associates and I were amazed at how many youths and men said they 'did not mind prison'. To them, it became a place of refuge. Their friends were in prison or had been in the past; the food was regular and, in comparison with what they had before, of good quality; in the words of one prisoner, 'there were few fights and few hassles'.

The fact that prison was seen as a safer place than the reserve says much about the success of government policies which have attempted to create Aboriginal 'communities'. But no real community existed from the start. Simply moving people into a common housing area does not create bonding or a viable social grouping. As the Peters know so well, such policies reinforce the sense of futility and alienation that individuals and families feel.

7 The Official Weapons

On Powerlessness and Prejudice

At the core of the debate on Aboriginal matters is the issue of power and powerlessness. The question is, who should have the power to decide where and how indigenous Australians live? In Australia, particularly in Queensland, the answer to this question has long been known by both blacks and whites. During a confrontation between Premier Joh Bjelke-Petersen and Aboriginal reserve councillors in August 1981, one councillor, interrupting the Premier's dismissal of any claim by Aborigines for freehold land, said, 'We are worried about our people. We've been told for the last 200 years what is good for you and now we want to say what is good for us'.

But what is good for Aborigines has never been seriously considered by Australian politicians, particularly by those from Queensland. The World Council of Churches were astonished to discover during their 1981 study tour of Queensland Aboriginal reserves and settlements, that the Queensland Premier refused to meet them. The Council delegates, in touring Queensland, were attempting to compile information on Aborigines that would be useful in framing constructive proposals.

The Council of Churches were even more startled to find themselves described as a 'communist front' and as 'agitators' by the Queensland Government. Despite having on its six-person panel visiting Australia such distinguished Christians as Pauline Webb, Vice-President of the British Methodist Conference, Bjelke-Petersen preferred to listen to other Christians.

Among Church leaders who were welcomed in 1981 by the Premier was an American fundamentalist preacher, Dr Carl McIntire, famous for once denouncing President Richard Nixon as a 'pinko'. Dr McIntire's organisation, the International Council of Christian Churches, presented their own report on

Aborigines to the Queensland Government. In that report, McIntire and his colleagues suggested that 'sin and alcohol' were behind most of the problems confronting Aborigines.

The denigration of the World Council of Churches' Report and the active encouragement of fundamentalist Christian spokesmen who support government policy is just one tactic used by the authorities in rationalising their policies on Aborigines. The Department of Aboriginal and Islander Advancement continues this policy and often uses choice phrases of 'endearment' to describe their opponents.

In the 1979 Department of Aboriginal and Islander Advancement Report, these tactics are made abundantly clear. The report notes, 'This campaign of denigration and deception (about the Government's policy on Aborigines) comes almost entirely from outside Queensland and that, regrettably, prominent among the promoters are Commonwealth agencies and their officers'. The 1980 report comments that 'Australia has increasingly been held to ransom by a few Aborigines with well developed political techniques'.

The denigration does not end there: further on in the 1980 report these 'very few' Aboriginal activists are described as a 'motley collection of opportunists and social misfits seeking the political, financial or emotional advantage that is the reward of a shrewd manipulation of Aboriginal people'.

Aborigines stereotyped in this way are vilified both in and outside parliament. Townsville activist, Shorty O'Neil was, according to the Queensland Minister for Aboriginal and Islander Affairs, Ken Tomkins, a 'white fella'. Further, according to Tomkins, Shorty O'Neil 'earned an income as a professional Aborigine'.

Queensland Ministers are happy to distinguish between 'black fellas' and 'white fellas' for political vilification, no such difference is recognised when public policy is considered. While researching this book, I attempted to obtain figures on Aboriginal crime, court appearances and imprisonment from Queensland Government Departments. It was impossible to obtain these figures from the Departments and they severely questioned the wisdom of keeping such statistics. Indeed, Government policy is one of smug satisfaction about the fact that figures are not kept on Aborigines.

This policy is proudly stated in the 1980 Department of Aboriginal and Islander Advancement Annual Report: 'It is a sign of success of the policy', the report says, 'and the attitude towards integration that on electoral rolls, hospital and social service registers and business books, no special records of indigenous people are maintained'.

It is this very 'attitude towards integration' that keeps blacks and whites, ignorant about the extent and nature of the social problems that confront reserve dwellers. Information is power, and ignorance means powerlessness. The Queensland Government minimises the former and maximises the latter when dealing with indigenous people.

In the subjugation of a defeated people, two forms of maintaining power emerge. The first is by what Bernard Smith has called 'a psychological control' — a process in which the victors suppress their moral doubts concerning the more brutal facts of conquest. The second, epitomised by Queensland Government policy, is the dominance of the laws of the victors over the laws of the vanquished.

In the administration and control of Queensland reserve communities, past policies and practices are still being carried out. Aboriginal people are 'managed', in a total sense, by government officials who retain the powers and responsibilities for the 'well being' of Aborigines.

Such powers and responsibilities are, as we will see, considerable. Rowley compares those who live under these powers on reserves as similar to writer Alexander Solzhenitsyn's image of Soviet prison camps, as expressed in his novel, *The Gulag Archipelago*. The reserves are institutions, spread throughout the State but virtually invisible to all but their inmates.

Despite reserve councils, Aboriginal police, consultation with government officials and public relations practices, control of the reserves and the destiny of their inhabitants remain firmly with white bureaucrats and white politicians. The managers run the reserves, the departmental officers draft the legislation and the politicians decide on the overall fate of the people.

That power ultimately resides in Brisbane and not with the people on the reserves is clear from the official record. As we have seen, the people of Mapoon had no say about their houses being burnt down or about being forcibly transported to Weipa. When the people of Aurukun and Mornington Island rejected a proposed State Government takeover, and voted to remain under the administration of the Uniting Church, the Government introduced the Local Governments (Aboriginal Lands) Act of 1978.

Under this Act, the reserves were turned into local government shires, thus effectively removing the Uniting Church administra-

The Peter's house at Weipa South.

tion. Not unnaturally, both these communities now fear the large-scale intrusion of bauxite mining companies. The Mapoon story may well be forgotten by whites, but blacks in all areas remember it well.

Alwyn Peter was unable to take his destiny into his own hands. His family was forced by government officials to move from their home to a government reserve. While on that reserve, Alwyn was controlled by white managers, and by-laws that were made by a race and a culture alien to his own. Whether he got a job, lived in a house or received unemployment benefits was determined by white men using the authority of white laws. He may not have liked whites, but Alwyn was respectful towards them. They, after all, had the power.

This power is evident in other places besides Weipa South. Every Queensland reserve operates under a set of laws and by-laws that effectively take control of a person's life and place it under white authority.

Craig, in his analysis of the effect of Queensland policy and laws on the people in Yarrabah, arrived at a similar conclusion. He found that at Yarrabah, the community's by-laws (which the reserve police and the local Justice of the Peace are bound to uphold) rarely represent the community's view. Although the reserve was originally created to isolate Aborigines from white society, it was changed to a training camp to prepare the people for the Queensland Government's grand plan of integrating blacks into the general community. The by-laws were designed to pursue that policy, not to reflect the interests of the reserve dwellers as a whole. But, as Craig's research demonstrates, the effect of the by-laws is that the Department of Aboriginal and Islander Advancement is seen as controlling everything that happens in the communities. This control leads in turn to a psychological dependency: the people believe that the Department will and should take care of every aspect of their existence.

Such psychological dependency is not unusual when one group oppresses another. Terrence Des Pres in his analysis of life in the Nazi concentration camps reaches a similar conclusion. In the horror of the death-houses, people went meekly to their fate, believing that resistance was impossible. Similarly, Elkin, in his study of southern plantations and American slaves, observed a pattern that remarkably parallels life on Aboriginal reserves. Absolute power creates truly child-like behaviour involving utter and abject dependence on the oppressor.

In both the concentration camps and the southern American plantations, similar mechanisms were used by those in power to denigrate the powerless, in much the same way that Aborigines have been denigrated by white Australians. Both Des Pres and Elkin note that people were degraded, made to appear less than human, their very souls assaulted by terror and privation. Aborigines may not be confronted in the same direct way, but equivalent processes occur. Power is denied to them, their identity stripped by policies of 'integration' and their culture and traditions deliberately dismantled.

When the Aboriginal people are reduced to a drunken, brawling race — a picture that is constantly fed to white citizens — it is much easier to treat them as inferior beings. They are therefore not worthy of assistance, power or human empathy. Just as the Nazis found that degrading Jews made mass murder less terrible to the murderers, so too does white Queensland find that the degradation of black people assists in rationalising our paternalism and indifference, and the immorality of assimilationist policies.

One final comment should be made on the effect of power and dominance. As Des Pres and Elkin discovered in the concentration camp and in the plantation, it was commonly observed that the outcome of powerlessness was hostility to life itself. The violence that is the hallmark of Aboriginal communities, the senseless self-mutilation that characterises men and women and the purposelessness that epitomises the lives of Alwyn, Harold and all the others, are very similar to the disrespect for life described by Des Pres and Elkin.

One reason white liberals are so apathetic about the position of Queensland Aborigines is the almost bland account given to students about Queensland's native people. Robert Armstrong, in his history of the Kalkadoons, has noted that even university textbooks ignore basic facts about Aboriginal social life. Histories often stress that Australia was occupied peacefully, ignoring the fact that the Native Mounted Police of Queensland were organised on military lines.

Until fairly recently, university courses in anthropology were full of discussions about Aboriginal kinship systems and rituals but were almost mute when it came to describing their political powerlessness and legal oppression. Queensland liberals often voice their sympathies towards Aborigines, but rarely take political action or give concrete assistance.

The Queensland media, as with the Liberal and Labor Parties, present no alternative to the National Party view and continue the desecration of Aboriginal culture. Indeed, I have heard senior ABC television reporters say they would not do too many stories on conditions in Aboriginal reserves because of 'all the flack we get from the government'. The gap between the media's sympathy towards Aborigines, and their achievements, is considerable.

However, the Queensland Government and its Department of Aboriginal and Islander Advancement must take most of the blame for the apathy of Queenslanders about Aboriginal affairs. Those who criticise Government policy are referred to as 'trouble-makers'. If they work at tertiary institutions, the full force of the Government's resources is pitted against them, ensuring that research information or even access to Aboriginal areas is denied. Even more importantly perhaps, basic information about crime, health and other aspects of Aboriginal existence is denied to all but government officials. Secrecy and slander are the twin weapons used by the Queensland Government in their continued denigration of Aboriginal culture.

The inability of Aborigines to influence their own destinies is not just confined to Queensland. New South Wales, a State which has been dominated by Premier Neville Wran and his Labor

Party machine, has been consistently criticised for doing nothing to improve Aboriginal self-determination. A bi-partisan State parliamentary report called attention to the deplorable physical and psychological environment in which most of the 45,000 Aborigines of New South Wales live. The report urged the rejection of the old policy of assimilation and its replacement by self-determination, recognising that the dependent, institutionalised status of Aborigines has not changed significantly since colonial days.

Indicative of this trend were the remarks of Kenneth Quinn, Stipendary Magistrate in the far-west NSW town of Wilcannia. In sentencing a local 20-year-old Aborigine for use of unseemly words, Quinn told the convicted man that he was a member of a race of pests. Specifically, Quinn, in giving an opinion of the behaviour of Aboriginal people in the town, said, 'Your race must be (the) most interfering race of people I have heard of. You are becoming a pest race in Wilcannia wanting to interfere in (the) job of police. There is only one end to pests. Learn this time'.

Even the Federal Government, which preaches self-determination for African States and bemoans the policies of the Queensland and Western Australian Governments on Aboriginal affairs, is more concerned with public relations than pragmatics. Despite all the Federal Government's rhetoric and threats, it has backed down on every important issue when confronted with an intransigent Queensland Government. The Commonwealth itself does little. Only 7.3 per cent of the entire Aboriginal workforce is employed by the Commonwealth; Qantas has only two Aborigines on its staff of 13,000. None of the departments in Parliament House employs any Aborigines.

It is in Queensland, however, that the powerlessness of Aborigines can most clearly be seen. This powerlessness does not exist in a vacuum, but flows instead from the deliberate policies the State Government has pursued over the past 100 years.

The Political Weapons

The policies of the Queensland Government towards indigenous people have been clearly if not precisely stated for a number of years. Premier Bjelke-Petersen, writing in the *South-Burnett Times* of 23 July 1980, said, 'the Government's goal has been to end the isolation of the original Australian and bring them into the mainstream of today's society'. According to the Premier, the people of Queensland 'look forward to the day when every Aboriginal and Islander Queenslander accepts the responsibilities which go with the rights of citizenship'.

The Premier was not able to spell out exactly what these responsibilities and rights were, but he was adamant that these rights did not include 'a return to the romantic past'. Nor did they include land rights. In a telling sentence, Bjelke-Petersen assured his supporters that the State Government 'upset radical activists and a few urbanised part-Aborigines because we will not grant...special and exclusive rights in land, minerals or anything else.'

Such sentiments are clearly shared by the Department of Aboriginal and Islander Advancement. In the Department's Annual Report, the Director, Mr Killoran, says, 'In Queensland this department will continue to consider the needs of the total Queensland community and to regard indigenous citizens as citizens of this State, not an elite group to be risked in the process of bold social planning'.

'Bold social planning' has never been the hallmark of the Queensland Government. Indeed, according to Killoran, 'Queensland Aborigines do not want to participate in a movement toward separate law, land, language and people, for this is to form a separate country'. But despite the Government's and the Department's assertions that Aborigines agree with their policies and co-operate with them, all does not appear to be as rosy as would seem. In a paragraph in the Department's 1979 Annual Report, we learn that some Aboriginal councils have wandered from the integrationist's path:

> It is a matter of great regret on the part of the Department and frustration on the part of residents that...councils have spurned the concept of partnership in favour of a course chiefly identified to date by rhetoric, conflict, confusion and inaction. Such a course is unlikely to provide the opportunity for a council to gain experience and confidence, or encourage the state government to view it as capable or worthy of exercising local responsibility.

Despite the constant assurances that the councils run their own affairs, here is a frank admission that this is not so. The implied threat that if the State Government does not have confidence in councils they will not therefore grant them 'responsibility' is obvious to both reserve residents and their councils. They have, after all, seen over a number of years the way the Aboriginal and

Torres Strait Islanders' Act operates, and are aware of who holds the power under the Act. It is not the residents or the councils.

Professor Garth Nettheim's analysis of the laws relating to Aborigines in Queensland demonstrates that the councils are completely subordinate to the management, just as managers, district officers and councils are all responsible to the Director of the Department of Aboriginal and Islander Advancement. Nettheim, in his attack on the Queensland legislation, points out repeatedly how sections of the legislation violate the Universal Declaration of Human Rights. For example, residents on reserves are subjected to a special court system regulating not only internal reserve matters but also issues that could be the subject of legal proceedings elsewhere in the State. Given this fact, Nettheim asks, how can Australia pay even lip service to Article 7 of the Human Rights Declaration which assumes that 'all are equal before the law'? Under Queensland laws, people cannot move freely on reserves, cannot buy houses or land, do not get paid award wages and cannot complain about their conditions.

Wages paid to Aboriginal workers on reserves are well below award wages. Unskilled labourers receive, in some instances, $58 per week, which is less than half the award wage. At Yarrabah, bulldozer operators are paid $82 per week when the industrial court has set an award payment of $150.64. All housing is owned by the Department and almost all business enterprises controlled by them as well. All staff on reserves are employed by the Department or by Church authorities. The lack of Aboriginal input can be seen by the fact that there are no Aboriginal managers or deputy managers on reserves.

Even the Aboriginal police are under the control of the reserve manager and their status and prestige seriously threatened by this fact. The police do not receive any formal training, and accusations abound that they are biased in favour of relatives and independent of community council control. The independence of the council itself, is, as the Commonwealth Commissioner for Community Relations points out, illusory. While the State Government has the ability to abolish individual community councils — which it has done in some cases — and keep the books of accounts of the councils, control is clearly in white not black hands. Yet the 1979 Department Report accused councils of not accepting full financial and administrative responsibilities! The councils know only too well that such responsibilities, to use Bjelke-Petersen's terminology, rarely involve rights.

The joint submission of the Aboriginal and Torres Strait

Islander Legal Services and the Foundation for Aboriginal and
Islander Research Action in 1978 surveyed people living on reserves in Queensland. From their sample, they located 22 people
who had been moved from one reserve to another against their
wishes. Indeed, under the 1965 Act, the Director of the Department or an authorised officer had the power to move a person not
living on a reserve, onto any reserve in Queensland, and to
transfer him from one reserve to another. Although repealed by
subsequent Acts, many people were subjected to its power.

    The ultimate question of who controls reserves and their future
lies with the Government and the Department. Many communities feel considerably anxious about their future rights of occu-
pancy, not without reason. As Nettheim notes, 'the termination
of the Aurukun and Mornington Island reserves by a stroke of a
pen will not have gone unnoticed in other communities'.

Typical hut on Mornington Island, North Queensland.

The Economic and Social Weapons

Despite the advances Aboriginal people have made in securing their own land in South Australia and the Northern Territory, in Australia as a whole they are still servants to large business enterprises. On Aboriginal land anywhere in the country, governments have never refused multi-national developers the right to exploit potential economic resources.

Despite the rhetoric by the Commonwealth Government about integrating Aborigines into the wider society, no federal government has passed legislation similar to that of former Premier Don Dunstan's Labor Government, for the Pitjantjantara people Indeed, both State and federal governments have been conspirators, in conjunction with multi-national companies, in ensuring that Aboriginal people are denied more land and prevented from having effective control of the land they already possess. There can be no doubt at all that governments, particularly in Queensland and Western Australia, have placed a far higher priority on capital investment than on Aboriginal protection.

In Western Australia, Amax Petrol, with a police escort, invaded Aboriginal land at Noonkanbah to allow mining to begin. When the multi-national conglomerate Tipperary wanted to mine alumina on Aurukun in 1979, neither the government nor the company thought to ask the people whether they wanted mining. Nabalco at Gove displayed similar insensitivity to Aborigines by breaking their promise to control waste disposal in Melville Bay. This led to catastrophic results for local fishermen when mass poisoning of fish occurred.

In the Northern Territory, Aboriginal people concerned about the decision on whether to mine uranium were taken by the Department of Aboriginal Affairs to Bouganville in order to assess the impact of mining. At Bouganville, the group were very impressed by the massive involvement of Aboriginal workers. But the delegation were not taken to Weipa or Mapoon where, as we have seen, the Aboriginal people were excluded from involvement in mining — indeed, where the people were forced from their land because Comalco wished to mine it.

The Ranger Inquiry was told by the then Director of Aboriginal Welfare that mining would lead to almost full employment of Aboriginal people living in the area. The Commissioners of the Inquiry believed the Director, and mining was allowed to begin. But, as Tomlinson and Davey point out, the mining operation has had no substantial effect on the 60 per cent unemployment levels of Aboriginal people in the areas. When some of the traditional owners attempted to use the courts to force Queensland mines to honour agreements made as part of the decision to mine, they were thwarted. The Minister for Aboriginal Affairs at that time, Senator Chaney, introduced retrospective legislative amendments preventing traditional owners from seeking justice through the courts.

It is at Aurukun, however, that we see clearly the way governments and mining companies join forces to exploit Aboriginal people. For despite the objections of the Aurukun people (together with the administrators of their reserve, the Uniting Church) to mining, the Queensland Government was able to override all opposition. When the Commonwealth Government joined forces with the people and the Church and refused to grant export licences to the mining companies until a satisfactory agreement was reached, it appeared as though the miners and the Queensland Government had lost.

However, in 1978, the Queensland Government checkmated its opposition by taking over the management of Aurukun and Mornington Island from the Church and subjecting both areas to the provisions of Queensland's Local Government (Aboriginal Lands) Act of 1978.

Under Section 30(1) of this Act, mining rights are specifically dealt with in that the granting of leases to the council still leaves the Crown all gold, mineral and petroleum rights including the free right of access for exploring, exploiting and transporting them. As Nettheim has argued, despite other Sections of the Act that treat shires as if they were still reserves for the purposes of mining — theoretically giving Aborigines some control of the right to mine — the Government retains full and effective control over mining operations.

According to the former Queensland Aboriginal and Islander Advancement Minister, Charles Porter, mining would go ahead at Aurukun no matter what. When in 1980 it appeared that mining at Noonkanbah would not begin, Porter was quick to announce that any delays in mining in northern Australia 'would have no effect on long-term plans to develop the bauxite deposits near Aurukun'. As it was, mining began at Noonkanbah as it will undoubtedly begin at Aurukun.

The Queensland Government also shows its contempt for Aboriginal rights in providing no legislation recognising or protecting Aboriginal sacred sites. Although the Government does have an Aboriginal Relics Preservation Act, and has classified nine sites under it, they are not, according to the Association of Professional Anthropologists and Archaeologists, sacred sites 'and have been declared because from a white point of view they look good'. The sites which have been classified are mainly rock engravings, art work or sacred trees because, 'whites are impressed by them as they associate the classified sites with an exotic past — the era of the noble savage'.

In contrast to the Northern Territory, New South Wales and South Australia, where laws recognise sacred areas, Queensland refuses to recognise areas of mythological significance such as rivers, mountains, creeks and water-holes. Even if a group of Aborigines wishes to buy an area in Queensland to preserve its spiritual and historical significance, the Queensland Government objects. The Aboriginal Development Commission, empowered to buy land believed sacred, has been able to purchase only a small number of blocks in Queensland because, in contrast to other States, the Government refuses to transfer the leasehold title of purchased lands to Aboriginal groups.

Behind these moves is always the concern on the part of the Queensland Government that Aboriginal land holdings would make mineral exploitation difficult. Although legal powers exist which would allow mining on Aboriginal reserves, the enforcement of these powers would undoubtedly be politically explosive. Not even the Queensland Government can afford to repeat the Aurukun and Mornington Island events. Consequently, suggested repeal of the Aborigines and Torres Strait Islander Act and revocation of the 50-year leases offered by the Queensland Premier were greeted with dismay by Aborigines.

The repeal of the Acts would pave the way to revoke the gazetting of reserve lands. Any leases drawn up would then avoid geographical areas with mining, tourist or forestry potentials. Although Aboriginal reserve lands make up only two per cent of the area of Queensland, they include sites of great tourist potential, areas of major interest to bauxite, uranium and tin mines, and contain fishing and forestry possibilities.

The World Council of Churches delegates were aware that neither State nor federal governments would protect Aboriginal claims to land. In their 1981 report, they said: 'Powerful multinational interests have already contrived with the States to deprive Aborigines of their rights . . . this alliance poses a serious threat to Aboriginal survival'. The brutally exploitative alliance between the Queensland Government and Comalco to rob Alwyn

Peter's forefathers of their land at Mapoon suggests that this prognosis is realistic.

But even in Mapoon, those that have taken the land justify their actions on the grounds of 'progress'. In the film, *Weipa People*, made by the Comalco company in 1979, a commentator notes that Weipa is 'the biggest bauxite mine in the world — a massive achievement'. The commentator then observes that 'a few years ago Weipa wasn't even on the map'. In a stunning piece of public relations fantasy, the Comalco manager described Weipa as 'a place people can call home'.

But who can call Weipa 'home'? It may be a home of sorts, no matter how temporary, to white workers. Many young men spend from a few months to a year at the mine making good money. It is extremely doubtful whether Alwyn, Maggie, Rachel, Sidney, or any other Aborigines who were forced from their traditional lands at Mapoon and made to settle at Weipa South would call it 'home'. But then, in a State hell-bent on development, it is not unusual for social myths to be substituted for social facts.

So it is with housing. Although the Queensland Department of Aboriginal and Islander Advancement proudly announces in their Annual Report that 'housing remains the base on which the government's policy of integration is being built', whole areas of Aboriginal communities in the State lack adequate accommodation. In Urandangie, outside Mt Isa, no camping or toilet facilities are available for about 30 people permanently living outside the town. Old car bodies and bushes used as windbreaks are the only protection available to people subjected to the harsh and cruel climate.

The north-west Queensland town of Camooweal has a fringe camp on its outskirts described by city council aldermen as 'atrocious and disgraceful' when they visited the site four years ago. In 1982, conditions remain the same. Four unpainted corrugated tin sheds serve as the only shelter for the families who live there, and each shed is in a dilapidated and depressing condition. They lack sinks and running water and some are without doors. Washing is done in communal laundries and drainage is non-existent. The stench from waste water in over-flowing drains is overpowering.

Even in Queensland's third-largest city, Townsville, 100 homeless Aborigines sleep on bare ground without shelter. Less than 100 metres away from a multi-storey, multi-million-dollar city centre, scores of Aborigines sleep under the Victoria Bridge. They complain of being constantly harrassed by the police and told to move on. According to Cathy Doolan and Hank Williams, two of the homeless, the police revel in raiding their temporary abodes. 'The police hound us no matter where we go' said Cathy, 'and when they find us there is always some sort of argument — if we've got a stew cooking they'll tip it over and if we say anything we'll be charged'. Hank Williams added that the police 'delight in doing things like that and while they're doing it they laugh their heads off'.

Inadequate housing on reserves, on fringe settlements or in towns is not only the result of uncaring bureaucrats or xenophobic policemen. It is related as well to the high level of racism among white Australians. In a little publicised but important study of discrimination against Aborigines in north Queensland, visiting American psychologist Knud Larsen and his associates conclusively demonstrated a deliberate prejudice by landlords against black tenants.

Larsen noted the way landlords and real-estate agents reacted to both black and white applicants seeking housing in Townsville. When the applicant was an Aborigine, it was generally found that the landlord requested a $200 bond. On the other hand, white applicants were only required to deposit a $100 bond for the same house. Similarly, landlords responded very differently to requests for information about accommodation vacancies. The usual response by landlords to Aboriginal tenants was to say 'some people have already taken it'. For whites, landlords would take down names and addresses, often phoning back the next day to offer accommodation.

Larsen perceptively points out in his study some of the reasons Aborigines do not complain about discrimination in housing and other aspects of social life. To begin with, who is there to complain to anyway? The Federal Community Relations Commission is one of the few bodies which can take action in the event of overt prejudice and discrimination in accommodation, hotel drinking or employment matters. But it is in Canberra and appears remote to an Aborigine already overawed by white authority.

Legal action or complaints to State government departments seem equally futile. The burden is largely on the Aboriginal complainant who is frequently without the personal resources to carry a protracted case through all the layers of bureaucratic barriers, including long delays. So most discrimination remains unreported. The apathy which indigenous Australians feel as a result of a lifetime of inferior status, real fear of repercussions from the white community, and a sense that nothing will be done anyway, all contributes to the low number of official complaints of discrimination lodged by Aboriginal people.

Justification for discrimination shown towards Aborigines by landlords or hotel-keepers generally centres on two arguments. The first suggests that Aborigines are unable to adequately look after houses or flats. The second, usually emphasised by hotel owners or licencees, stresses the fact that Aborigines cannot hold their liquor.

To take the latter point first, although the level of Aboriginal drinking is alarmingly high, the evidence we have accumulated in the course of researching this book suggests that Aborigines can hold their liquor just as well as whites. They may drink excessively, but so do whites, very few of whom are asked to leave hotels.

The housing issue is more complex. On reserves and in cities, Aboriginal people often damage their accommodation. Alwyn Peter and his brothers at Weipa South frequently kicked in walls or punched through glass louvres. But such behaviour partly resulted from the appalling conditions they were living under, which led in turn to profound despondency, frequently resulting in destructive acts.

In any event, closely clustered white housing is very different from the shelter and way of life Aborigines were used to. Native Australians were nomadic, coming together for festivals or ceremonies, then dispersing, then coming together again. They often saw no more than 20 people for most of the year and were used to low-density living. However, in most Aboriginal areas, housing is now in very short supply and most homes are overcrowded. Living within four walls, with many people sleeping in small, confined spaces, creates enormous psychological pressures. As anthropologist John Taylor notes, 'Much of the damage that Aborigines do to their European style house stems from their inability to cope with walls, windows and doors'.

Despite these facts, government officers still apply a behind-closed-doors approach to Aboriginal housing and cannot understand why Aborigines wreck or abandon their three-bedroom accommodation and live in humpies they build themselves. Open log-and-leaf houses with space for a number of families might well be preferable to the present approach. Such accommodation, if carefully designed, could cater for changing family structures by having walls that can be easily removed and placed elsewhere in the house according to need.

It is doubtful however, whether all or even most cases of dis-

crimination in housing result from a fear on the part of the landlords of accommodation being mistreated or wrecked. As with
employment, Aborigines are refused accommodation or jobs
simply because they are Aborigines. The World Council of
Churches were sensitive to the racist component inherent in individuals and in many Queensland Government policies towards
black Australians, and were quick to condemn it. 'Racism', they
said, 'is entrenched in every level of Australian society.'

Similar discrimination exists in employment opportunity. With
more than 17,000 Aborigines registered as unemployed at the
beginning of 1981, the unemployment level among blacks is six
times that of the general workforce. Given their relatively low
level of education, this is not surprising. About 25 per cent of
Aborigines never attended school; 43 per cent did not proceed
beyond primary school level; only 2 per cent reached matricula-
tion. The Federal Government has initiated special moves to
reduce these figures — in 1981, 2000 more Aborigines were given
jobs during a special three-month Commonwealth campaign —
State government assistance is seriously lacking.

In Queensland, preference is generally given to Torres Strait
Islanders, rather than Aborigines, for jobs on some reserves.
Even within reserves or shires, it is not uncommon to find outside
contractors building houses without employing local labour. On
Mornington Island, for example, housing construction was
completed without the use of local people despite a massive unemployment level in the shire.

In all areas, political, social and economic forces are brought to
bear on Aboriginal Australians, effectively denying them power
over their own destiny. Most Aboriginal leaders see traditional
culture as resilient and worthwhile, but they do not necessarily
wish to reconstruct or preserve a fossilised culture of the past, or
stop all development. What they want is a chance to control the
type and pace of development and a chance to restate, rather than
recreate, the traditions of the past.

8 Ending the Slaughter

A Country's Stigma

The Aborigines were once masters of the huge Australian continent. Now a once proud race of warriors, hunters and fishermen are very different. Languishing in prisons, captives of alcohol and drifting on the fringes of white settlements, tens of thousands of black Australians are the visible symbols of white man's progress. Alwyn Peter and his dead girlfriend Deidre were two victims who happened to capture media attention. But, as we have seen, there are many others who have been cast aside as Australians increasingly become obsessed with resource development and economic growth.

The death and mayhem we have observed in this book is partly related to this obsession. Products, it seems, have often come before people despite government rhetoric to the contrary. Although much of the face-to-face violence that has been portrayed here refers to blacks killing blacks, Aborigines do not live in a different context of violence from whites — only one that differs in quantity and in language. Whites use different words to describe this violence: when Aborigines were massacred during the colonisation of Queensland, the acts were simply described as 'frontier expansion'; when the people of Mapoon were forcibly evicted from their homes, the act was described as 'resettlement'; when Aboriginal lands are taken for mineral exploitation, the process is simply called 'development'.

It may be argued that guilt is a bad motivator for social action. Some have believed that to harp on the past misdeeds of citizens and governments in the treatment of Aborigines leads to rationalisation, suppression or misdirected action. Present conditions appear, by the standards of the past, to be so much better, so Aboriginal problems now have less impact.

But the past must be remembered if only because the present

can never really be understood without reference to it. In Xavier Herbert's magnificent novel, *Poor Fellow My Country*, Jeremy Delacy sums up the importance of remembering the past with these words:

> To me the Aboriginal problem is a fundamental one not only in this region where it's still a very important issue in every aspect of life here, but for Australia generally . . . because only the other day, in terms of history, we stole this land we've been so quick to call our own, stole it with murder and mayhem and about the lowest forms of meanness a human being could stoop to . . . and we have to reconcile the matter someday, either by acknowledging the fact that we're bloody-handed thieves and being proud of it, or giving back what we stole, and not as an act of charity, but of downright humility.

Most Australians, especially the Queensland Cabinet, do not acknowledge that they are 'bloody-handed thieves'. Neither would they acknowledge the responsibility that they bear in the acts of murder and self-mutilation that occur on Aboriginal reserves. But by taking traditional black homelands, by refusing to allow Aboriginal self-determination and by actively enforcing on Aborigines an assimilationist framework, we have subjected them to a fatal psychic trauma that manifests itself in alcoholism, self-effacement and self-destruction.

Federal Government policies have differed from their Queensland counterparts in some regards. The rhetoric of the Commonwealth has not been to enforce assimilation: on the contrary, for more than a decade, prime ministers and cabinet ministers have said Aborigines could accept or reject Europeanisation as they wished. In 1972, Prime Minister McMahon said 'The Government recognizes the right of individual Aborigines to effective choice about the degree to which, and the pace at which, they come to identify themselves with Australian society'. In 1974, the Federal Liberal–Country Party election policy stated the same sentiments. 'We recognize', they said, 'the fundamental right of Aborigines to retain their racial identity and traditional lifestyle or where desired, to adopt a partially or wholly European lifestyle'.

Despite this rhetoric, many Federal programs, as with their State counterparts, are, consciously or unconsciously, still directed to assimilationist purposes or at least designed to put pressures on Aborigines to seek to be assimilated. Dr H.C. Coombs has identified examples of this pressure, which include the demand by Federal departments that Aboriginal enterprises be conducted with the same motives of profit as white enterprise; the unwillingness of the Federal Parliament to use its legislative powers in Queensland in pursuit of its own stated policies; and the unwillingness to allow Aborigines a direct share of the financial benefits from mining on their land. These and other actions reinforce an assimilationist orientation and, in the words of Coombs, keep Aborigines 'a landless proletariat—dependent wholly and without alternative on wage employment or on charity'.

Despite their protestations to the contrary, the processes by which the Federal Government negotiates with Aboriginal groups contribute markedly to their 'landless proletariat' status. Philosophically, the present Federal Government's proclaimed policy of self-determination, self-management and land rights is the most enlightened that Australia has yet adopted towards the Aborigines, but in practice the philosophy offers nothing new. The terms of self-determination and self-management are still essentially white not black terms, and in matters of consultation, white procedures are invariably adopted.

Aboriginal societies are traditionally small autonomous groups which use specific areas of land, each with their own leaders, laws, sacred sites and body of knowledge. Consultation should, at the very least, be with these small autonomous groups so that people would be treated in their own terms and according to their own social organisations.

But, as Paul Albrecht has revealed, these facts of Aboriginal life are ignored. Aboriginal people are asked instead to elect representatives to speak to governments on their behalf — 'a white democratic process which cuts across their way of operating'. Both government and voluntary bodies continue to bring together Aborigines belonging to different districts and groups when matters such as federal funding, land rights and associated issues are negotiated. This process is distinctly alien to Aboriginal communities and it is therefore little wonder that the people rarely feel any commitment to what has been decided in these consultations.

The Federal Government's policy on self-determination and self-management has led in practice to the establishment of white bureaucratic and organisational structures with Aborigines filling the positions, in some cases, instead of whites, and making decisions on behalf of other black people. So what has changed? 'Nothing', suggests Albrecht, 'but the actors'. The Aborigine is

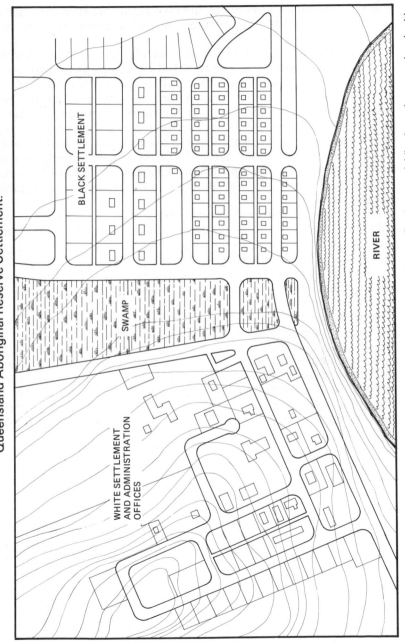

Queensland Aboriginal Reserve Settlement.

White accommodation: high ground, well planned, spacious, healthy. *Black settlement:* flood prone, rigidly planned, cramped, unhealthy.

still not treated as a person in his own right, because his organisations and traditional channels of communication are still ignored.

In the Northern Territory, despite much publicised land rights legislation, the same white-dominated communication processes prevail. Ten years ago a Federal Government committee chaired by Professor Gibb recommended that certain areas be excised from pastoral leases and given to Aboriginal communities. With about 30,000 Aborigines in the Territory and 243 pastoral leases, Gibb expected that large numbers of leases would be handed over to black people. However, after ten years of debate and negotiation following the Gibb report, only 10 small areas have been cut out of the giant pastoral empires and given to Aboriginal communities.

The Northern Territory's land rights legislation does not grant land on Aboriginal terms, but on white terms. The Territory Government has the power under the Crown Lands Act to resume 'any Crown Lands the subject of a lease . . . for the use and benefit of the Aboriginal inhabitants of the Territory', but the pastoral lobby has ensured that, so far, the legislation has never been used.

Besides, the Northern Territory land rights legislation does not envisage groups or clans obtaining direct title to their land. Instead, title is held by white-style land trusts and control is exercised through another structured organisation. Such structures appear bound to continue. According to recent reports, the Territory Government is hardening in its attitude to Aboriginal applications for land and Chief Minister Paul Everingham says he has been asked 'to bring some sanity to the application of land rights'.

The 'sanity' that Everingham wishes to bring to the Northern Territory has overtones of the 'sanity' that the Queensland Government has constantly applied to Aboriginal claims for land in that State. With an overtly assimilationist philosophy, the Bjelke-Petersen Government has consistently ridiculed black and white individuals who wish to see indigenous Australians acquire unencumbered land. The Premier and his ministers have constantly rationalised this decision by saying that they do not wish to have South African apartheid in Queensland.

Paradoxically, of course, the people of Weipa South, Yarrabah, and other reserves would argue that such a situation exists already in the north. The people, often forced to live in areas without traditional significance, are controlled by white bureaucrats and are living in conditions of squalor, disease and violence similar to those observed in Soweto. Despite the lack of official statistics, it is salutory to note that black settlements in South Africa have frequent outbreaks of drunken brawls, murder and self-destructive acts remarkably reminiscent of Queensland Aboriginal communities.

But the suggestion by the Queensland Premier and the Australian mining industry that land rights for Aborigines would resemble South African apartheid is deceptive in the extreme. If one looks at the realities of the apartheid system, the false comparison is obvious. In South Africa, 87 per cent of the land is reserved for the 20 per cent who are white. The average white income is about 10 times that of blacks, and political power is monopolised by whites through police-state measures, including imprisonment without trial, restriction of the Press, and outlawing of major black political organisations.

In Queensland, Aborigines make up two per cent of the population, have no representative in State Parliament and are among the poorest and most problem-ridden communities in the industrialised world. To suggest that the granting of land rights to this powerless minority would result in an apartheid system similar to that existing in South Africa is patently absurd.

Yet such thinking continues to dominate the Queensland Government. At the end of 1981, the dominant partner in the Queensland coalition, the National Party, had formulated another alternative to the soon-to-be-repealed Aboriginal and Torres Strait Islander Act. In the middle of 1981, the Party proposed a 50-year lease for Aboriginal reserves, an idea that not unexpectedly received much criticism from black people who were demanding freehold title.

In the face of this criticism, the National Party decided to propose freehold title for Aboriginal reserves but such title was to be given with caveats attached. For example, boards of trustees were to administer the lands, and the trustees would include representatives of State and Federal Governments. In addition, powers were to be conferred in the proposed legislation enabling mineral prospecting officers to search for minerals on the land. According to the Party policy, if vested bodies used the land for criminal purposes it would be taken away.

Such proposals make a mockery of the claim by the National Party that Aborigines will be able to control their own land. Would, for example, the Cattlemen's Union be satisfied if grazing land was held in trust by boards with State and Federal representatives? And if Aborigines tried to stop individual prospectors or multi-national corporations from exploiting the land and the people, would this constitute, in the eyes of the Queensland Government criminal activity?

Let us imagine that marihuana was discovered on Aboriginal land. Does that mean that the land could be seized by the government and the entire Aboriginal community dispossessed? Despite massive raids by police on north Queensland marihuana plantations, I cannot remember one case where any of the land on which the plant was grown was forfeited to the Crown. Why then, should it be any different for Aboriginal land?

Clearly the National Party proposals have the familiar ring of a 'father knows best' philosophy. There was no consultation with the Aboriginal communities in Queensland when the proposals were drawn up. If they had consulted these communities, they would have found, as the Aborigines and Torres Strait Islanders Legal Services found, that 98 per cent of all Queensland Aborigines wanted an inalienable community title to each reserve.

It is debatable whether the lessons of history have been learnt and deliberately forgotten in Queensland, or simply not noticed. The State has, as we have seen, a record of treating its Aboriginal population with contempt and at times brutality. The result of forcing its policies of assimilation and white control on indigenous people has, directly and indirectly, adversely affected the lives of almost all reserve Aborigines. This process must be reversed by denouncing paternalism and by supplanting it with policies that stress self-determination and self-control.

New Directions

Aboriginal problems are many and therefore there is no single new direction. Indeed, to talk about 'the Aborigines' is itself misleading. Instead, we are looking at a diverse people with multifaceted problems. Consequently, the search for universal panaceas to the issues raised in this book — such as better housing, health or education — is dangerously simplistic. These measures, with perhaps 100 others, could be effective if applied simultaneously, but the reality is that this will never happen. Besides, such panaceas lack a conceptual or philosophical base that would give a framework to any new directions suggested.

Such a conceptual or philosophical framework does exist, however, and its roots can be found in Stanner's work, *After The Dreaming*. Stanner argues that homelessness, paternalism and, perhaps most of all, powerlessness are the fatal elements in Aboriginal life. Aborigines are homeless because they have no stable base of life: 'Every personal affiliation was lamed; every group structure was put out of kilter; no social network had a point of fixture left'.

Paternalism is the hallmark of Queensland approaches to Aboriginal issues and has, with every Act, deepened 'the poverty into pauperism and the dependence into inertia'. Powerlessness, so often discussed in this book, is a condition which has lasted from four to eight generations, effectively crippling initiative, self-respect and identity.

So homelessness, paternalism and powerlessness are elements to be overcome in any initiatives designed to help Aborigines. They will not be overcome cheaply. To give just one example, the purchase of land to provide traditional Aborigines with a spiritual home is a highly expensive proposition. Federal funding for such ventures has recently been increased — the Aboriginal Development Commission received $47.8 million this financial year compared with $23 million last year — but much more money is needed. The Development Commission may well have had an increase in funds, but the Aboriginal people are now $213 million short of the assistance promised by the Fraser Government in the 1975 election.

The National Times calculated that, taking into account the effects of inflation over the past six years, this accrued loss is the equivalent of almost two years of funding for all Aboriginal people. In specific areas, the 1981–82 budget represents a decline in real terms of 42.8 per cent in housing funds, 22 per cent for health funding and 30 per cent in education when compared with the Whitlam Government's spending on Aboriginal projects.

As important as funding, however, is the direction that philosophies on Aboriginal issues take. Land rights are perhaps the greatest single issue confronting Aborigines when problems of homelessness, paternalism and powerlessness are considered. So Australians must have a commitment to granting certain Aboriginal communities a clear, unencumbered right to traditional lands. Nowhere is this more important than on the Cape York Peninsula, where the Queensland Premier has announced his plan for a wilderness park.

Under those plans, mining activities will continue and might be expanded. Grazing will also continue but in the long term, properties will be purchased and declared national parks. Both on the Peninsula, and in other parts of the State, the Government will follow its clearly set down policy of integrating Aboriginal and Islander people within the general community.

Anthropologist Bruce Rigsby has demonstrated conclusively that the entire Peninsula is divided up into literally hundreds of named countries by their Aboriginal owners. These include ceremonial grounds, fighting grounds, native wells, camping sites and totemic centres. The Peninsula is not an unknown wilderness to its Aboriginal owners. Instead, it is part of them, and Aboriginal people now speak of it as their country and their home. People who were born on reserves, even if they have never visited the Peninsula, still identify themselves as belonging to their fathers' (and fathers' fathers') country of origin. According to Rigsby, Aboriginal people on and off the Peninsula 'have never stopped talking about their loss of land'.

However, with the Queensland Government's wilderness policy for Cape York, Aboriginal reserve land and other traditional areas are likely to become national parks in the management of which the Aboriginal people will play little or no part. All of this will effectively destroy any attempts by Aborigines to own land in the areas which have historical and spiritual significance for the people.

A model solution to this problem can be found in the reports of Mr Justice Woodward of the Aboriginal Land Rights Commission. Referring to the Northern Territory, Mr Justice Woodward recommended that Aboriginal people should obtain land in three ways: firstly, by the Federal Government transferring existing reserves to Aboriginal ownership; secondly, by Aboriginal groups laying claim to unalienated Crown Land before a judicial commissioner; and, thirdly by an Aboriginal land fund purchasing land on the open market.

Despite the failure of the last recommendation in Queensland — the State Government refuses to transfer leases to the Aboriginal Land Fund Commission — the other two measures have direct relevance for Queensland. The first would mean that the Aboriginal people would be given freehold title to present Queensland reserves without boards of control or any other conditions. In addition, the Queensland Government should cease forthwith refusing the transfer of leases to Aboriginal groups so that those who are traditional owners and/or have historical associations with the area can buy relevant blocks of land. In the event of a dispute over what is 'relevant', a federal commissioner, with anthropologists and Aborigines, should decide on the claim. It should not be forgotten that most of Queensland's Aborigines want ownership of reserve lands to be in their hands and wish the Commonwealth to replace the State Government as the body responsible for making laws.

Unequivocal land rights under these conditions would enable the diverse Aboriginal communities in Queensland to exercise the choice of how they wish to control their future. Thus, with development — say, mining — Aboriginal groups would vary according to whether they allow it and would be able to vary the pace at which they allow development to occur. As in the Northern Territory, Aboriginal groups would assess mining projects in terms of what they wanted at a particular time. No form of development would be acceptable to all or even most groups. However, freehold title to land would enable each community to make locally-based decisions according to the wishes of the people at the time, thus alleviating the problems of homelessness, paternalism and powerlessness.

These problems have also to be overcome in the provision of health facilities and services. In previous Chapters of this book we have seen that deaths by violence and by disease on reserves are among the highest recorded in the world. In spite of the money allocated by both Federal and State Governments and the operations of huge public service bureaucracies, mortality and morbidity rates remain horrendous. All reasoned medical opinion, including that of former flying doctor Howard Stevens, suggests that Western-style, symptom-based medicine does little to alleviate the basic health problems in Aboriginal communities. Indeed, community health problems can more often be attributed to community psychological problems than vice versa. Overcoming these problems can only begin when Aborigines are able to control their own destiny and resources.

A major step in this direction would be the Aboriginalisation of medical facilities. Studies of Aboriginal usage of medical services, even in cities and towns, have shown that Aborigines prefer to be treated at Aboriginal-controlled medical clinics rather than in the more impersonal health systems operating in white Australia. Despite the resounding success of these clinics in New South Wales, the Northern Territory and in other parts of the country, the Queensland Government has done virtually nothing to take this direction.

Dr Coombs, among others, has pointed out that the removal of hygiene and nutritional deficiencies among Aborigines could save white Australians a lot of money. The most important changes needed to substantially reduce the mortality and morbidity experienced by Aborigines are new nutritional practices and public hygiene procedures. Supply of water, sanitation and shelter are the most important hygiene factors. But progress will only be made when the nature and pace of new facilities and procedures are in black not white hands. The quantity and quality of such services are now dictated by whites, who tend to see the provision of housing, sewerage and water supplies on Aboriginal reserves as a cost. This attitude contrasts markedly with the provision of basic infrastructures in cities and country towns — such expenditure is generally seen as investment.

To enact the policy of increasing the degree of power Aborigines exert in their own affairs and reducing paternalism, substantial changes will have to be made to the procedures adopted in Aboriginal communities to enforce social control. We have seen elsewhere in this book that Aborigines have un-questionably been very harshly treated by the Australian criminal justice system. The Australian Law Reform Commission is now grappling with the issues of how and where Aboriginal customary law should be adopted.

One weakness in the Commission's frame of reference relates to its over-emphasis on criminal law matters to the exclusion of 'personal law' areas. Questions relating to marriage, dissolution of marriage, child custody, title to property and a host of related matters are critically important in Aboriginal social organisa-tion, which differ markedly from white organisation.

On criminal law, the position taken by the Law Reform Com-mission appears to be that customary law should be retained only in traditional areas, which limits its application to about five per cent of all Aborigines throughout the country. In most of the reserves mentioned in this book, customary law therefore could not be introduced, as Europeanisation of the communities has progressed too far. The failure of European criminal justice to control or reduce the amount of violence on reserves is abundant-ly apparent. Aboriginal police and courts on reserves are equally ineffective, cutting across traditional decision-making proce-dures and lines of authority.

David Weisbrot has suggested that customary law should not be seen as static, but rather as a dynamic entity constantly changing according to social conditions. This view contrasts with the more fixed view of traditional law taken by the Australian Law Reform Commission, and allows customs and dispute-settling procedures to change according to circumstances. Thus custom is not frozen or codified, but rather adapted to time and place.

If this more fluid, dynamic approach to the question of the adoption of customary law were applied to Queensland Aborigines, far more than five per cent of the black population could use customary law procedures if they saw fit. This law may be modified from that operating in traditional times, or it could be a combination of customary and Western law. But if reserve communities decided themselves on exactly what the law should be, and enforced it themselves, it is very likely that social cohesion and control on Aboriginal communities would improve and that violence would be reduced.

The overseas experience indicates that when customary law is simply grafted onto Western courts, little use is made of traditional laws and customs in practice. The ambivalence of Western-trained lawyers and judges towards traditional laws, the supremacy of case law and the strict laws of procedure and evidence in Western courts make it very difficult for traditional law to emerge, let alone predominate in any court decision. If we are serious about coming to grips with Aboriginal powerlessness, homelessness and paternalism, we will be a lot more effective if we allow Aboriginal communities to set up their own dispute-settling and social-control procedures.

A precedent for some of these procedures exists in other countries. In Israel, the individual must designate the religious/customary regime that will be applied to him or her in personal law matters. In New Guinea, there is a well developed system of village and land mediation courts; in the United States, native American Tribal Courts are well established. Legal pluralism is an accepted philosophy that appears to work well.

However, my suggestions go beyond most of the procedures proposed or practised in this country or overseas. I would not limit the scope of Aboriginal control and criminal justice methods to minor offences, nor restrict them only to traditional communities. If we are really serious about rekindling an Aboriginal identity — perhaps a different identity from that of the past — it is important that they control the nature of dispute-settling procedures including those that involve violence or crime against individuals and groups within their communities.

The objections to this proposal are many. It has been argued that this legal pluralism will open the floodgates for other minority groups within Australia to demand their own criminal justice system. No such move for this step is readily apparent at the moment and besides, if one emerges, it will have to be dealt with on its merits. The objection relating to the position of urban Aborigines is similarly weak. If offences are committed outside Aboriginal-owned areas, they should be dealt with by European courts. The view that Aboriginal communities have cruel and harsh punishments — spearing, for example — is a value judgement rather than a statement of fact. To some Aborigines, protracted prison sentences are an infinitely worse form of hell than a short but painful spear through the thigh.

It is highly unlikely that the sentences given by European courts to violent offenders from Aboriginal reserves in Queensland have done anything constructive to reduce anti-social acts and to increase community cohesion. Alwyn Peter's court appearance and subsequent prison sentence, for example, appeased few within Weipa South and was so far removed, both geographically and socially, from the reserve, that its effect was almost certainly lost. If, on the other hand, Alwyn and other offenders had been dealt with by effective procedures devised by the Weipa people themselves, more positive results for the community might have been achieved.

In other areas, the same basic philosophy of increasing Aboriginal self-management and reducing white paternalism must be followed. Dr Coombs correctly noted that few schools in Australia teach anything substantial about the environment within which Aboriginal children live. 'Rarely', says Coombs, 'is any serious attempt made to integrate the teaching of the school with the educational practice of the Aborigines themselves.' Not surprisingly, therefore, many teenage Aborigines are often 'rootless, idle and destructive'.

In white schools, many textbooks are racist in content and generally ignore the history of white exploitation and conquest. References to Aborigines are sometimes still cast in the 'noble savage' context and unduly romanticise the living conditions of urban and rural black people. Serious analysis of the sociological and economic conditions of indigenous Australians is generally lacking and black and white alike receive a superficial knowledge of Aboriginal culture and history.

More Aboriginal-controlled schools for black communities are urgently needed, particularly at the pre-school and primary levels. Self-esteem and racial pride will only flow when young people have a chance to explore their own history and recognise the intricacies and delights of their own language and customs.

Powerlessness and paternalism begin in the classroom and can be substantially reduced by creative educational practices derived and controlled by the Aboriginal people themselves.

In 1967, almost 90 per cent of those who voted at the referendum declared that the Commonwealth should have full power to legislate for all Aboriginal citizens. The exact message inherent in this massive vote is unclear, but it is probable that most Australians were asking for a better deal for native Australians.

That better deal has not yet eventuated. Fifteen years later, the Federal Government is still not prepared to negotiate a treaty or 'makarrata' with Aborigines which both acknowledges that Australia was first occupied by Aborigines and that they were the original owners of the land. In Queensland, no thought of such a treaty has ever been contemplated nor will be in the forseeable future.

Despite the violence on reserves, little notice has been taken of the mistakes of the past. At Yarrabah in December 1981, the Queensland police threatened to abandon policing the reserve because in recent years all but one of 12 officers posted there ended up in hospital. The police union described Yarrabah as the most violent place in Queensland and demanded more men to enforce law in the community. More law they felt, would mean more order.

These simplistic solutions were not accepted by Aborigines. Robert Smallwood, a member of the Aboriginal Council at Yarrabah, said that the reason for the trouble was that Aborigines do not have control of their own affairs at the reserve. According to Smallwood, 'the Aboriginal Council has no real power, as all the important decisions are made by the Department of Aboriginal Affairs in Queensland...the Aboriginal people need total control of their own affairs to restore their self-esteem'.

No such control will be forthcoming. However, political leaders could well observe the operation of the outstation movement in the Northern Territory, South Australia, Western Australia and even Queensland, where a real attempt by Aboriginal people to restore their self-esteem is starting. During the past decade, large numbers of Aborigines have been leaving mission stations and government settlements in these States to establish small villages on their traditional lands.

These hamlets have come to be generally known as 'outstations' and they number about 200 with a total population of about 6000. In general, the movement back to traditional home-lands has been led by adults in the upper age range. One language is usually spoken by the members of a community, which is made up of traditional owners, their spouses and other close relatives.

Although the main source of cash income for the outstations is social security payments, some communities are supplementing their incomes by vegetable growing, fishing and other enter-prises. Most outstations depend in varying degrees on hunting and gathering, although the diet is generally a combination of traditional and European foods. In many places, an extensive re-affirmation of traditional religion occurs, often combined with Christian practices and principles.

The most encouraging development from the outstation move-ment, however, is that the communities 'are more peaceful than the settlements and missions and that morale is better'. Obser-vers have noted that stress and tension, so common on reserves, are substantially reduced in outstations, and that the pride and bearing of the men improve dramatically. Early evidence suggests that attempts at self-management and self-control, and efforts to regain a more traditional physical, social and spiritual environment, have been very successful. Unfortunately, the Queensland Government's unrepentantly paternalistic outlook towards the Aborigines makes it unlikely that the lessons of the outstation movement will be applied widely in that State.

Since 1788, only British law applied to the colony and this im-plied that Australia was a settled and not a conquered colony. In contrast to the settlement of America and New Zealand, land in Australia was, and still is, considered vacant because no civili-sation was recognised and no Aboriginal law noted.

With the gap between the average real conditions of Aborigines and white Australians widening, not narrowing, it is imperative that real attempts are made to reduce the levels of powerlessness and homelessness experienced by black Australians. Only measures incorporating self-control and self-management of the type described in this Chapter will have any chance of doing that.

9   A Choice of Futures

The Chain of Violence

Alwyn Peter was not the first and certainly will not be the last Queensland Aborigine to kill girlfriend, wife, sister or father in a moment of rage. Two weeks after Alwyn was sentenced by Mr Justice Dunn, two Aborigines from communities in north Queensland followed Alwyn Peter into the dock at the Brisbane Criminal Court charged with killing a lover or a relative.

One was called Russell. This 17-year-old from Mornington Island savagely beat his 16-year-old girlfriend and then drowned her. The crime, described in detail in Chapter 2, was committed while the youth was heavily intoxicated and when he was experiencing extreme jealousy.

Russell's case crystallises those elements of black violence that we have discussed in this book: forced settlement, fragmentation within and between communities because of the crime, and a lowering of self-respect and self-esteem among Aboriginal people generally.

Russell's maternal grandmother, with her sisters, their children and other members of the family, were moved in the early 1930s from Turn-Off Lagoon in Queensland's gulf country to the mission on Mornington Island. However, when food resources were scarce on the Island during World War Two, the mainland people on Mornington Island were forced to move again, to either Doomadgee or Aurukun.

Russell's mother's mother went to Aurukun and settled there with all her children. While at Aurukun she married a second time, and her daughter, Russell's mother, also married an Aurukun man — the father from whom Russell took his surname.

Although the girl who was killed was not related by blood to Russell's family, most of her relatives lived at Doomadgee. When a person dies under such violent circumstances in a community other than the one where most of the family live, tensions often arise between the two peoples. Such tension, it appears, manifested itself after the death, between the communities of Mornington Island and Aurukun.

As with other cases, the ramifications of black violence are more far reaching than at first realised. Shortly after Russell killed his girlfriend, Larry Lanley, the Chairman of the Mornington Island Shire Council, died. Lanley was Russell's mother's elder sister's son — his 'cousin-brother' or 'brother' in local Aboriginal parlance. Lanley's death was perceived by his and Russell's extended family to be, in part at least, connected with the death of Russell's girlfriend.

As a result of Lanley's death, his family at Mornington Island became profoundly depressed. But the family also had relatives living at Doomadgee and mourning occurred there as well, including acts of self-mutilation by Lanley's mother and by other family members. Thus three communities, Mornington Island, Aurukun and Doomadgee were affected in adverse ways by one act of violence.

These events were not related at Russell's trial, although his background, including experiences similar to those of Alwyn Peter, were pointed out by the defence. However, when sentencing Russell, Mr Justice Williams asked the Public Defender, Bill O'Connor, to tell him where in all the Aboriginal violence in northern Queensland, alcohol was not involved. Neither the Public Defender nor the Crown prosecutor could give an example of a non-alcohol-related violent crime.

Mr Justice Williams appeared confident that alcohol lay behind Aboriginal violence and said, 'It's drink all the way'. The Judge then observed that Aborigines had been good workers 'until given access to liquor and other monies' which, he said, took away the incentive to work. The law, it appeared, together with the prohibitionists, were both sure that behind all evil lay the demon drink.

But explaining Aboriginal violence through alcohol grossly over-simplifies a complex chain of events which have profound historical and cultural significance. In a sense, this book has been about this chain of events. The reasons Aborigines drink so heavily relate directly and indirectly to the destruction of traditional Aboriginal society that began when the first settlers landed in Australia. This destruction continues, perpetuated by politicians greedy for development, by community 'leaders' cocooned complacently in Australian suburbia, and by an insidious

racism that pervades much of the Australian population. Like it
or not, most of us can share the blame for the alcoholic black
person we see stumbling down the streets of Townsville, Brisbane or Weipa South, and the man who sits quietly in the dock
charged with killing his girlfriend.

The Past Repeated

During Alwyn Peter's trial, and to some extent during Russell's
court case, testimony was presented relating to historical and
social factors associated with living in Queensland's black communities. In the former case, the displacement of people from
their homelands, the appalling social and economic conditions,
the high morbidity and mortality rates and other factors relevant
to Alwyn Peter's psychological and sociological state were
dissected, analysed and triumphantly produced. The trial allowed
experienced Brisbane barrister, Des Sturgess, and his resourceful
solicitor, Peter Clapin, to mount a sustained argument on
Alwyn's behalf.

But the experts they paraded before the courts and the facts
that these experts produced, had a real touch of 'deja vu' about
them. Somehow, somewhere, it seemed as though it had all
happened before. It had, in Queensland, in a small country town
called Cunnamulla in the south-west of the State. In that town 14
years ago, an Aboriginal woman named Nancy Young was
charged with the manslaughter of her four-and-a-half-month-old
daughter, Evelyn.

The grounds of the manslaughter charge were that Nancy
Young had failed to provide her daughter with adequate food and
failed to seek medical attention. After three months spent in jail
after being unable to raise bail, Nancy was found guilty by an all-
white, all-male jury and sentenced to three years hard labour.
Her appeal was heard but dismissed by the Queensland Supreme
Court. After a further two months, during which media and television coverage of the case was incessant, the full Supreme Court
reversed its decision on the grounds of fresh evidence and freed
Nancy, one month before she was due to be released on parole.

During the trials and hearings, it became apparent that Nancy
Young's alleged negligence occurred as a result of the appalling
social conditions of the Queensland Aboriginal community in
which she lived. She shared a tiny tin shack with four adults and
ten children; the nearest supply of water came from a tap 40

yards away from the house; unsewered and fly-covered earth closets were the only sanitation provided; infectious diseases were rife and deaths by tuberculosis and pneumonia were common.

Attitudes by the Cunnamulla townsfolk were predictably uncaring, and at times, actively racist. Despite an admission by the local Council Health Inspector, a Vietnam veteran, that 'the conditions here are in many respects worse than the conditions which exist in refugee villages in Vietnam', more money was spent by the Council on the town cemetery than on the Aboriginal reserve.

During her daughter's short lifetime, Nancy Young received child welfare payments and part-time waitressing wages averaging six dollars a week. This was the amount, two writers about the case observed, 'which the law was to insist that she "adequately" feed herself and her children'. As with the children of Maggie Don and Rachel Peter, Nancy Young's offspring were plagued by disease and institutionalisation. At the time of Evelyn's death, poverty had forced five of Nancy's children into child welfare institutions; another had long since died; one was living with relatives; and two (both with a history of illnesses) were living with her in the crowded tin hut.

Although Nancy Young was charged with neglecting her child, her real crime was, in the words of Robertson and Carrick, 'to be coloured, poor and occasionally tipsy, to breed without benefit of clergy a swarm of children who brought the offensive odour of the reserve into the local hospital once too often'. Her crime became worse when media publicity flaunted Cunnamulla and the attitudes of its residents in front of the entire nation.

As with Alwyn Peter, Nancy Young became a 'cause celebre'. Both received enormous publicity which highlighted the injustices and the appalling social conditions under which they lived. Both were freed or given light sentences. In the case of Nancy Young, her original conviction was eventually quashed; for Alwyn Peter, a recommendation for immediate parole was handed down. Both, however, were given justice for the wrong reasons.

Nancy Young had her conviction quashed on the grounds of 'fresh evidence'. The evidence consisted only of two medical experts' testimonies suggesting that a disorder of body chemistry, rather than deliberate neglect by Nancy, was the probable reason for Evelyn's sudden dehydration and eventual death. However, this evidence was heard only after considerable publicity from television programs, such as Four Corners, which pointed to the shocking conditions under which Aborigines lived at Cunnamulla. Nancy Young was set free, but the evidence failed to come to grips with the real cause of the original injustice — the treatment of Aborigines in Queensland.

As with Nancy Young many years earlier, Alwyn Peter suddenly became a 'cause celebre' and was dealt with leniently. Nothing much was said by the court about the white hands that lay behind the death of his girlfriend Deidre, and most of the other deaths that occurred on Aboriginal reserves.

In sentencing Alwyn, Mr Justice Dunn, as with judges before and after him, made much of Aboriginal drinking problems. Taking into account the 21 months that Alwyn had been in custody awaiting trial, Mr Justice Dunn imposed a 27-month sentence with a recommendation that Alwyn be immediately considered for parole. In passing sentence, the Judge said that Alwyn had been very drunk when Deidre was stabbed. Consequently, he considered it correct that the Crown accepted Alwyn's plea of guilty to manslaughter rather than murder.

According to Mr Justice Dunn, 'The evidence also shows that whilst alcohol is usually the trigger which releases violence, there are other factors to take into account. It is indeed because of those factors that so much uncontrolled drinking takes place'.

These other factors were never specified by Mr Justice Dunn, although in his judgement he found the expert evidence by anthropologists, psychiatrists and sociologists 'thought provoking' and 'illuminating'. Much of this expert evidence considered the historical factors associated with white settlement and the social and political conditions existing on Queensland Aboriginal reserves.

It is these 'other factors', not specified by the Judge nor by anyone alse in authority, that really affect black violence. It may be useful for Alwyn Peter to undergo an alcohol rehabilitation program — a condition of his parole — but nothing will be changed for black people on reserves by focussing on one individual to the exclusion of Aboriginal communities as a whole.

This lesson is one which Queensland and Australia should have learnt by now, but have not. Sociologist Jackob Najman analysed all Australian deaths by homicide over a three-year period to ascertain the causes of murder and manslaughter. Najman's research demonstrated that homicide rates in Australia are low in comparison with other countries, but some groups in the community report murder and manslaughter rates which are extremely high. In particular, Najman found that persons with the lowest occupational status are much more likely to be victims of homicide than people with high-status occupations. He concluded that the 'causes' of homicide are economic and social deprivation and a sense of powerlessness among groups from which offenders came.

Najman's study demonstrates the futility of a punishment-oriented approach to the problem of murder and manslaughter. Policies which rely on more police and longer prison sentences simply do not take into account the social or structural causes of violent death. Says Najman, 'The need for a harsher punishment philosophy is unlikely to lead to any significant change in the incidence of homicide'. Reduction of the homicide rate would require 'a reduction in economic inequality' and 'an improvement in social conditions generally'.

The lessons from his research for the incidence of violence on Aboriginal reserves are clear-cut. Aboriginal reserve dwellers are probably the poorest group in Australia. Their homicide and serious assault rates are among the highest in the world and the gap between their living conditions and those of most white people is considerable.

It is therefore most unlikely that more police — white or Aboriginal — or longer prison sentences will make the slightest difference to the Aboriginal violent crime rate. Improvement calls for measures which reduce economic inequality between black and white people and increase the self-respect of Aborigines and their autonomy in their own communities.

A Man Called Alwyn Peter

Let us consider Alwyn Peter's future in the light of what has been said about the causes of violence. To begin with, it is abundantly clear that if Alwyn Peter returns to Weipa South his propensity to violence will, in all probability, continue.

Psychiatrist Ivor Jones suggested during the trial that if Alwyn went back to the same or to a similar community with equivalent pressures on him and similar social forces operating, he could commit further violent offences against people. Jones' prognosis is not unduly pessimistic given the rate of repeated violence by the same offenders discussed in Chapter 2.

Matt Foley, a most experienced and astute observer of Aboriginal affairs, also believed that if Alwyn was returned to Weipa

South, major problems would occur. Faced with the same depressing, alienating environment, with the antagonism felt towards him by Deidre's relatives, violent confrontations were very likely to happen.

Foley recommended that Alwyn should return to Mapoon after serving his sentence. As Foley says, 'There are obvious problems associated with the proximity of Weipa South, but both in regard to the availability of his family support there and in relation to his own patterns of identification, Mapoon appears to be one place which he does identify as home'.

Repeatedly, in the weeks preceding his trial and during the trial itself, Alwyn said that he wished to return to Mapoon. His love of the land of his ancestors was obvious to all who met him. In my last meeting with him in Brisbane, this sentiment was expressed again.

On Friday 8 January 1982, with researcher Robyn Lincoln, I visited Alwyn at Boggo Road prison. When Alwyn arrived he looked fit and fresh. He had lost the glazed look that characterised him in the months after Deidre's death, and he greeted us with warmth and enthusiasm. This previously quiet and introspective man displayed an openness and charm that amazed both of us.

Although Mr Justice Dunn had recommended immediate parole, the Queensland Parole Board had not yet released him from prison. As is the Board's practice, no reason was given for this decision, but the fact that he was still in prison did not unduly disturb Alwyn — he was, he said, 'a very patient man'.

He told us that he was spending his time in Boggo Road writing poems, of which many were about his love for the land at Mapoon. He said that he wished to return to his traditional home but had heard that after his release from prison and the alcohol rehabilitation centre at Jodaro, it might be possible for him to obtain a job on a farm outside Cairns. Although this possibility excited Alwyn, he was still firm in his resolve to eventually settle at Mapoon.

Alwyn seemed extremely healthy in body and mind. He had put on weight and spoke vigorously and with conviction. Prison, it seemed, had not caused him pain or grief. Although he was extremely bored with life behind four walls, the last 18 months had at least dried him out after 15 years of heavy drinking.

But what was this physical and psychological improvement really going to achieve in the long run? Was it simply going to make him fit enough to continue heavy drinking when he was released from jail? Or would there be a real change of heart, a determination to build a better life for himself and his family?

Robyn Lincoln and I agreed that the odds were against Alwyn constructively changing his life. Mapoon, the land he loved and identified with, might well shorten these odds and offer a new lease of life and a new beginning. But would Weipa South do the same — or Cairns or, for that matter anywhere else in Queensland? It is, I think, extremely doubtful, and so for Alwyn, as for many others, the chances of a return to the vicious cycle of heavy drinking, violence and prison are considerable.

So what are we as a community to do about the Alwyns, the Oscars, the Russells, and all the others who kill and maim? We have a choice of futures, I would suggest, and one which will have to be resolved with some haste if we wish to stop once and for all, the killings that have plagued Queensland Aboriginal communities.

The first choice is to continue with the piecemeal reforms of the past. Over the past 20 years, governments of all political persuasions have attempted to improve Aboriginal health, housing and education. They have as well, appointed advisory councils, given a handful of black people middle-management positions in government or quasi-government bodies and congratulated themselves on the amounts of money spent on Aboriginal affairs.

But in Queensland very little has changed. The destruction and killing continues unabated. Nancy Young's child died in a hospital at Cunnamulla; Deidre was knifed on a government-owned reserve at Weipa. Only the faces of the young children who die prematurely, or the names of the women and men who are murdered by their de facto spouses, have changed.

We have, it seems to me, a second choice — one which requires considerable courage to implement but one which offers a real chance for the future. This second choice does not rely on small, piecemeal reforms, with injections of money controlled and administered by white bureaucrats. Nor does it rely on the 'helping' professionals, whether they be prison officers, social workers, or well-meaning but often misguided psychiatrists. There may well be a place for these people, but the services they offer will make little difference to the alienation Aborigines feel on reserves and communities.

The second choice centres on the right of Aboriginal people to determine their own future and to own their own land, unencumbered by white officials and white rules. It provides the motivation and the resources for black people to decide for themselves the life they lead.

Alwyn Peter's history and Deidre's untimely death teach us that we really have no choice. The only course that we can take is to eliminate our paternalism, increase Aboriginal decision-making powers and provide black people with their own land. Only then can we begin to erase from our collective conscience the guilt of all those black deaths that have, directly and indirectly, flowed from our white hands.

Notes

Chapter 1: Black Death

Death of Deidre
Page 2 par 1

Tom Wakefield's opening statement is taken from the trial transcripts of *R v Peter*, p. 1.
Alwyn's statement was taken from the Police Records of Interview, collected by Peter Clapin for the Public Defender's Office.
Alwyn's statement is taken from the trial transcripts in *R v Peter*, p. 77.

Page 2 par 4

Des Sturgess' opening statement is taken from the trial transcripts of *R v Peter*, pp. 8 & 9.

More Death
Page 3, par 2

Most of these observations come from newspaper accounts or accounts of violence among Aborigines in historical analyses of black–white contact. See, for example, Saunders, K., et al., *Exclusion, Exploitation and Extermination: Race Relations in Colonial Queensland*, Australia and New Zealand Book Co. Ltd, Sydney, 1975.

Page 3, par 3

These dossiers consisted of Police Records of Interview; summary statements from legal assistants; Comparative Sentence reports; reports by social workers, and supporting details taken over the phone or from newspapers. The extent of information provided in each case varied considerably.

Page 3, pars 4–5

The Public Defender had enormous difficulty in obtaining these records. Separate documents were not previously kept for Aboriginal and Islander offenders. So every name on file was checked out to determine its origins. As well, many private lawyers who were contracted by the Public Defender's Office did not send summary statements in regularly. (Aboriginal and Islander offenders are now clearly identified in these records).

In addition, anthropologists and professional people working on reserves have told me that fights occur daily in Aboriginal communities. These fights, however, are often stopped by relatives or friends, or the local police arrest the participants and place them in the lock-up overnight, with no formal charges laid.

Page 3, par 6

The dossiers contained 23 murder and manslaughter charges, 16 accounts of grievous bodily harm, and 43 cases of unlawful wounding and assault occasioning bodily harm. Anthropologists have cited to the author other incidents of violence known to them, that were not included in these dossiers.

The 17 Aboriginal communities included reserves, shires and country camps. They were: Aurukun, Mornington Island, Georgetown, Mt Isa, Weipa South, Palm Island, Doomadgee, Edward River, Gorge Mission, Yarrabah, Hopevale, Hughenden, Normanton, Mareeba, Innisfail, Cherbourg and Lockhart — eight reserves, two shires and seven country reserves.

Page 4, par 1

Content and computer analysis of the dossier cases were tabulated and statistically compiled with reference to the characteristics of the offenders, the crimes and the communities involved.

Page 4, pars 2–3

Queensland homicide rates were taken from the Police Commissioner's Report 1980–81, State Government Printer, Brisbane, 1981.

Page 4, par 4

Australian and international violence rates were taken from Mukherjee, S., *Crime Trends in Twentieth-Century Australia*, George Allen & Unwin, Sydney, 1981.

United States cities' rates for homicide and serious assault were taken from the *FBI Uniform Crime Report for 1978*, in the Police Information Almanac, US Government Printer, Washington, 1981.

See also Cohen, F., Chappell, D., & Wilson, P., 'Aboriginal and American Indian Relations with the Police', in Chappell, D., & Wilson, P. (Eds), *The Australian Criminal Justice System*, Butterworths, Sydney, 1972.

Page 5, par 1

Taken from the Queensland Police Commissioner's Annual Report for 1980–81, op. cit.

Page 5, pars 2–3

These cases of multiple violence came from the dossier cases, Murder and Manslaughter File, pp. 32–63 & 354, Grievous Bodily Harm File, pp. 175–239, and relationships were verified by the Public Defender's Office and social workers involved.

Page 5, par 4

Details of Oscar's case history were taken from social work reports by Anne McKinnon, of north

Queensland, and collected by Peter Clapin for the Public Defender's Office. They were found in the dossiers in the Murder and Manslaughter File, p. 354 ff.

Page 6, par 1-2   Details of Oscar's case history, op. cit., p. 358.

Page 6, par 3   Oscar's statement was taken from the Police Records of Interview contained in the dossiers, op. cit., p. 361.

White Hands
Page 7, pars 1-2   The multifaceted nature of violence has been widely discussed by a number of philosophers and social scientists. An excellent account of the dimensions of violence can be found in Schur, E., *Our Criminal Society*, Prentice-Hall, New Jersey, 1969.

Page 7, par 3   A detailed history of the Aborigines in Tasmania can be found in Ryan, C., *The Aboriginal Tasmanians*, University of Queensland Press, Brisbane, 1981.
                     See also Armstrong, R., *The Kalkadoons: A Study of an Aboriginal Tribe on the Queensland Frontier*, William Brooks & Co., Brisbane, 1981, p. 176 ff.

Page 7, par 4-5   Ibid., p. 176.

Page 8, par 1   Letter by J.H.C. in *Moreton Bay Courier*, 16 August 1858, quoted in Reynolds, H., 'Racial Thoughts in Early Australia', *Australian Journal of Politics and History*, 1974, 20, p. 47.
                     The Queenslander, 18 October 1876, p. 18.

Page 8, par 1   Howe, M.B., *Aborigines and Christians*, Leader Press, Brisbane, 1977, p. 7.

Page 8, par 2   Armstrong, R., op. cit., p. 18.

Page 8, par 3   The history of dispossession in Queensland can be found in Roberts, J. (Ed.), *The Mapoon Story by the Mapoon People*, International Development Action, Fitzroy, Victoria, 1975.

Page 8, par 4   Estimates of the number of Aborigines and the number of reserves and communities were taken from: Department of Aboriginal and Islander Advancement (DAIA) *Annual Report*, State Government Printer, Brisbane, 1980-81; Department of Aboriginal Affairs (DAA), *Annual Report*, Australian Government Printer, Canberra, 1977-78 to 1980-81.

Page 8, par 5   These estimates also agree with those made by Nettheim, G., *Victims of the Law: Black Queenslanders Today*, George Allen & Unwin, Sydney, 1981.

Page 9, par 2   Gilbert K., *Living Black: Blacks Talk to Kevin Gilbert*, Allen Lane, Melbourne, 1977, p. 14.

Chapter 2: Killing My Brother

Who, How and Why?

Page 10, pars 1-2	Domestic violence is common in white communities and is far greater than official figures suggest. Research by Wilson, Scutt and others suggests that marital violence occurs in all sections of society and among all age groups. However, much middle-class violence is not reported to the police. For a detailed discussion of this research see Wilson, P., *The Other Side of Rape*, University of Queensland Press, Brisbane, 1978; Scutt, J., 'Spouse Assault', *The Australian Law Journal*, 54, 1980, pp. 720–31; and Scutt, J., *Domestic Violence in Australia: An Overview of Completed, Current and Projected Research*, Australian Institute of Criminology, Canberra, 1980.
Page 10, par 3	Much has been written about customary law. A good discussion of the use of specific punishments in the case of unfaithful women can be found in Bell, D. & Ditton, P., *Law: The Old and the New*, Central Australian Legal Aid Service, Canberra, 1980. In cases involving retribution or redress in traditional society, the onus was on the individual to obtain justice. The tribe would ensure that the individual carried out this action. In contrast to white society, no criminal justice superstructure of police and courts existed, so the individual carried responsibility for redress. This individual approach to justice may be found in some cases of violence today, particularly in instances where European criminal justice systems do not cover wrongs or misdeeds, e.g., infidelity.
Page 10, pars 4 ff	Figures on the relationship of the offender to the victim were taken from the dossier cases of Police Records of Interview, Murder and Manslaughter File, pp. 24 & 62, and also from social work reports collected by Peter Clapin for the Public Defender's Office.
Page 11, par 2 ff	Details of Percy's case history were taken from social work reports by Anne McKinnon, Murder and Manslaughter File, pp. 191–242 collected by Peter Clapin for the Public Defender's Office. Other examples were taken from the Police Records of Interview in the Murder and Manslaughter File, pp. 13 and 160.
Page 12, par 2	Taken from the analysis of the dossiers, op. cit.
Page 12, pars 3-4	Other weapons identified included rocks, bricks, broken flagon bottles, axes and a broom handle. These weapons were usually close by, indicating the spontaneous nature of the violence.

Page 12, par 5 ff   An objection to my argument is that the firing of a
                           gun or rifle requires little physical force or effort,
                           and yet its lethality is never questioned. But when I
                           looked at the full descriptions of these cases — and
                           in particular variables of weapon used; amount of
                           physical force; intent of offenders and subsequent
                           behaviour – and compared these with the results of
                           the violent actions, there was little doubt in my
                           mind that the death of the victim was often
                           unintended.

Page 12, par 5   From the statistical analysis of the dossier cases,
                           op. cit., Murder and Manslaughter File, pp. 1, 148 &
                           270.

Page 13, par 2   From social work report by Anne McKinnon, op.
                           cit., Murder and Manslaughter File, pp. 148 & 192.

A Pattern Repeated
Page 13, par 4   From the dossier cases, op. cit., confirmed by the
                           Public Defender's Office and the social worker for
                           Weipa South.

Page 14, pars 1–2   From Rachel Peter's statement contained in
                           Defence Witnesses' Statements Volume III, p. 21,
                           and from Alwyn Peter's Statement, Volume, II,
                           p. 6, collected by Peter Clapin for the Public
                           Defender's Office.

Page 14, par 3   Personal communication from Peter Clapin and
                           from social work reports contained in the dossier
                           cases, op. cit., Murder and Manslaughter File,
                           pp. 90 & 221.
                           From defence witness statement by Geraldine in
                           the trial of Harold, contained in the dossier cases,
                           op. cit., Murder and Manslaughter File, pp. 35–37.

Page 15, par 1 ff   From social work report by Anne McKinnon, op.
                           cit., Murder and Manslaughter File, p. 217.

Page 15, par 4   It is not uncommon for violence to be accepted as
                           the usual way of solving disputes in working-class
                           communities. What begins as a 'bit of a belting' can
                           often escalate into serious assault or death. See
                           Kutash, I. L., et al., *Violence Perspectives on
                           Murder and Aggression*, Jossey-Bass, San
                           Francisco, 1978.

People Who Kill
Page 16, par 1   Senator Neville Bonner at seminar prior to Alwyn
                           Peter's trial, organised by the Public Defender's
                           Office, Brisbane, 5 September 1981.

Page 16, par 2   From dossier cases, op. cit., Grievous Bodily Harm
                           File, p. 108.

Page 16, par 3   The dossiers contained frequent mention by judges

	of these two elements, Murder and Manslaughter File, p. 26. Alcohol particularly was mentioned. See, for example, Mr Justice Williams' judgement in the trial of Russell Pamtoonda, mentioned in Chapter 9 of this book.
Page 16, par 4 ff	Taken from social work report by Anne McKinnon, contained in the dossier cases, op. cit., Murder and Manslaughter File, pp. 323–35. Accounts of Russell's case were also reported in detail in the *Courier-Mail*, 2 October 1981, p. 3.
Page 17, par 4 ff	Chris Anderson and David Trigger from the Anthropology Department of the University of Queensland were consulted. They rated each criteria on a three-point scale ranging from high through medium to low. These ratings were then correlated with violence ratings calculated for each reserve in our study.
Page 18, par 4	From statements contained in Defence Witnesses' Statements Volume III, pp. 1–27 & 100–05. See also Roberts, J. (Ed.), op. cit., p. 15.
Page 18, par 5 ff	Taken from social work report by Anne McKinnon, contained in the dossier cases, op. cit., Murder and Manslaughter File, pp. 191–242.
Page 19, par 1	Ibid., pp. 32–63.
Page 19, par 2 ff	Ibid., Unlawful Wounding File, pp. 232–34.
Page 19, par 4	Roberts, J. (Ed.), op. cit., pp. 5–10.
Page 19, par 5	Taken from private communication from the D.A.I.A. Director (P. Killoran) to the Public Defender's Office, 18 August 1981.
Page 20, par 1	Joyce Charger speaking at seminar organised by the Public Defender's Office, Brisbane, 5 September 1981. Don Egan, former Weipa South reserve manager, speaking at seminar, ibid.
Page 20, pars 2–4	Figures in these paragraphs were taken from a statistical analysis of the dossier cases, op. cit. These paragraphs were also constructed from statements by Rachel Peter; hospital and other medical records; and the social work reports contained in the dossier cases, op. cit.

Chapter 3: Self-Mutilation

Another Form of Violence

Page 22, pars 1–2	From statements contained in Defence Witnesses' Statements Volume III, pp. 90–99, and social work reports contained in Reports Volume V, pp. 5–16, collected by Peter Clapin for the Public Defender's

	Office. Also found in Matthew Foley's social work report prepared for the Public Defender's Office, p. 7.
Page 22, pars 3-4	From Rachel Peter's statement contained in the Defence Witnesses' Statement Volume III, collected by Peter Clapin for the Public Defender's Office, pp. 19-20.
Page 22, par 5	Ibid., pp. 16-17.
Page 23, par 1	Taken from social work report prepared by Matthew Foley for the Public Defender's Office, p. 5.
Page 23, par 2	From Rachel Peter's statement, contained in the Defence Witnesses' Statement Volume III, op. cit., pp. 22-25.
Page 23, par 3-4	Ibid., pp. 18-19.
Page 23, par 5	Taken from Alwyn Peter's Statement Volume II, collected by Peter Clapin for the Public Defender's Office, pp. 26-27.
Page 24, par 1 ff	Ibid., pp. 26-28.

A Common Occurrence

Page 25, par 1	From Raymond Peter's statement contained in the Defence Witnesses' Statements Volume III, op. cit., p. 98.
Page 25, par 2	From background material prepared by Anne McKinnon contained in Reports Volume V, op. cit., pp. 36-37.
Page 25, par 3	Note that this list contains only one instance in which a female mutilated herself. She is Alwyn's sister, Amy. See pp.0 & 00 of this Chapter for further discussion.
Page 26, pars 1-3	From Amy Peter's statement contained in the Defence Witnesses' Statements Volume III, op. cit., pp. 73-74.
Page 27, par 1	From Ella Wymara's statement contained in the Defence Witnesses' Statement Volume III, op. cit., pp. 165-67.
Page 27, par 2-4	From Stephen Parry's statement contained in Defence Witnesses' Statements Volume III, op. cit., p. 114.
Page 27, par 5	From Don Egan, former manager of Weipa South, and social worker, Matthew Foley, in private communications with the author.
Page 28, par 1 ff	Matthew Foley, social worker at the University of Queensland, in private communication with the author.

Page 28, par 3	Rosser, B., *This is Palm Island*, Australian Institute of Aboriginal Studies, Canberra, 1978, p. 53.
Page 28, pars 4–5	Howard Steven's statement is taken from the trial transcripts of *R v Peter*, Day I, p. 28.
Page 28, par 5	Ivor Jones' statement is taken from the trial transcripts of *R v Peter*, Day IV, p. 253. Alwyn also sustained severe injuries in a car accident while he was unlawfully using the vehicle.
Page 29, par 1	Taken from a report by John Taylor prepared for the Public Defender's Office, contained in Reports Volume V, op. cit., p. 65.
Page 29, par 2	John Simon in private communication with the author.
Page 29, pars 3–4	Taken from John Goodin's statement contained in the Defence Witnesses' Statements Volume III, p. 191.
Old Customs Page 30, par 1	A thorough literature search revealed many references to self-mutilation in traditional society but virtually no mention of such behaviour in present Aboriginal communities.
Page 30, par 2	Frazer, J., *The Golden Bough* (3rd Ed.), MacMillan, London, 1976, p. 84.
Page 30, par 3	Ibid., p. 85.
Page 30, par 4 ff	Ibid., pp. 90–93. Weller, A., *The Day of the Dog*, George Allen & Unwin, Sydney, 1981, p. 68.
Page 31, par 2	Frazer, J., op. cit., p. 91.
Page 31, par 3	Ibid., p. 92.
Page 32, par 4	Jones, I., 'Stereotyped aggression in a group of Australian Western Desert Aborigines', *British Journal of Medical Psychology*, 1971, 44, pp. 259–65.
Page 32, par 5	Professor Stanner has written perceptively and compassionately about Australian Aborigines. Among his many books and articles one is of particular relevance for issues raised in this book. See *After the Dreaming*, The Boyer Lectures, Australian Broadcasting Commission, Sydney, 1968. The present statement comes from his comments prepared for the Public Defender's Office, contained in Reports Volume V, pp. 107–08.
Page 33, par 2	Harry Eastwell's statement is taken from the trial transcripts of *R v Peter*, Day IV, p. 216.

Page 33, par 3   It is relevant to note that since the first prisoners moved into the newly opened Jiko-Jika maximum security wing of Pentridge jail in September 1980, a series of violent attacks, bizarre self-multilations and a murder has occurred. The analogy between a maximum security prison and a Queensland Aboriginal reserve is probably unfair, but similar psychological and sociological pressures exist in both communities. See *The National Times*, 22–28 November 1981, p. 9.

Page 33, par 4   The literature suggesting a connection between frustration, aggression and suicide is considerable. See, for example, Wallace, J., et al., *Suicidal Behaviour*, Pergamon Press, Oxford, 1972.

Page 33, par 5   Jones, I., 'Diagnosis of Psychiatric Illness Among Tribal Aborigines', *The Medical Journal of Australia*, 19 February 1972, p. 246.

Page 33, par 6 ff   Much of the information contained in these paragraphs comes from residents and observers of reserves. Particular thanks are due to Pat Noonan and Rose Colless for information supplied.

Page 34, par 3   Ibid.

See also Bell, D., & Ditton, P., *Law: The Old and the New*, Central Australian Aboriginal Legal Aid Service, Canberra, 1980.

Page 34, pars 4–5   Pat Noonan, from The Alcohol and Drug Dependence Service, Mackay, in private communication with the author.

Chapter 4: Death of the Dreamtime

Life Before Whites
Page 35, par 1   Beaglehole, J. C. (Ed.), *The Life of Captain James Cook*, A. & C. Black, London, 1974, p. 514.

Page 35, par 2   Quoted by Widders from an unnamed Aborigine. It is interesting to note that when asked to describe Aboriginal society today, an elder of the Maris tribe in New South Wales replied by saying, 'A flagon, a couple of dozen bottles of beer, and a deck of cards. That'd be about it'. See Widders, T., in Stanbury, P. (Ed.), *The Moving Frontier*, A.H. & A.W. Reed, Sydney, 1977, p. 87.
Quoted in Smith, B., *The Spectre of Truganini*, The Boyer Lectures, Australian Broadcasting Commission, Sydney, 1980, p. 17.

Page 36, pars 1–2   See also Woolmington, J., in Stanbury, P. (Ed.), op. cit., p. 27, for a further discussion of the Dreamtime.

Page 36, par 3   From the family tree of the Peter family, prepared

	by Anne McKinnon for the Public Defender's Office, and contained in Introduction Volume I, p. 3.
Page 36, par 4 ff	From background material prepared by Anne McKinnon and John Taylor for the Public Defender's Office Contained in Introduction Volume I, pp. 1–27, and in Reports Volume V, pp. 58–67.
Page 37, pars 2–4	Ibid.
Page 37, par 5	Roberts, J. (Ed.), *The Mapoon Story by the Mapoon People*, International Development Action, Fitzroy, Victoria, 1975, p. 6.
Page 37, par 6	Ibid., p. 6.
Page 38, par 1	Ibid., p. 7.
	Amstrong, R., *The Kalkadoons: A Study of an Aboriginal Tribe on the Queensland Frontier*, William Brooks & Co., Brisbane, 1981, p. 176.
Page 38, par 2	World Council of Churches Report, *Justice for Aboriginal Australians*, Australian Council of Churches, Sydney, 1981, p. 8.
Page 38, par 3	Clapin, P., *A Chronological Account of the Life Story Of Alwyn Peter*, unpublished manuscript, Brisbane, 1981, p. 1. The dismantling of traditional Mapoon society is described in Roberts, J. (Ed.), op. cit.
Page 38, pars 4–5	The events are described in detail in Roberts, J. (Ed.), op. cit., pp. 16–18.
Page 39, par 1	Ibid., pp. 8 ff.
	From statements by Rachel Peter, Maggie Don and others contained in the Defence Witnesses' Statements Volume III, collected by Peter Clapin for the Public Defender's Office.

The Process of Destruction	
Page 39, pars 2–3	Roberts, J. (Ed.), op. cit., pp. 11–20.
Page 39, par 4 ff	Ibid., pp. 8–14. From Defence Witnesses' Statements Volume III, op. cit., pp. 100–05. Clapin, P., op. cit., pp. 1–27.
Page 40, par 5	From Rachel Peter's statement contained in Defence Witnesses' Statements Volume III, op. cit., pp. 12 ff.
Page 40, par 6	Roberts, J. (Ed.), op. cit., p. 14.
Page 40, par 7	Clapin, P., op. cit., p. 7 ff.
Page 40, par 8	From Alwyn Peter's Statement Volume II,

| | collected by Peter Clapin for the Public Defender's Office, pp. 2–5.
From Maggie Don's statement contained in Defence Witnesses' Statements Volume III, op. cit., p. 101. |

Page 42, par 1   From social work report prepared by Matthew Foley for the Public Defender's Office, p. 9.

Page 42, par 2   From statements contained in Defence Witnesses' Statements Volume III, op. cit., pp. 89–91.

Page 42, par 3   From Rachel Peter's statement contained in Defence Witnesses' Statements Volume III, op. cit., pp. 11–14.

Page 42, par 4   Roberts, J. (Ed.), op. cit., p. 3.
From Alwyn Peter's statement taken from the trial transcripts, Day I, p. 78.

Page 42, par 5   From transcripts of interviews between Delphine Geia and Sylvia Monk, Townsville, 16 October 1981.

Page 42, par 6   From transcript of interviews between Shorty O'Neil and Sylvia Monk, Townsville, 16 October 1981.

Aboriginality: What is Left?

Page 43, par 2   Langton, M., 'Urbanizing Aborigines: The Social Scientists' Great Deception', *Social Alternatives*, 1981, 2, p. 16.

Page 43, par 3   Ibid., pp. 16–22.

Page 43, par 4   For a discussion of urban Aborigines, see Langton, M., op. cit., pp. 16–22.

Page 43, par 4   From statements contained in Defence Witnesses' Statements Volume III, op. cit., pp. 158–67.
Clapin, P., op. cit., pp. 6–20.
Personal interviews with these women.
From statements taken from the trial transcripts, Days II – IV.

Page 44, par 3   Comments on women came from personal interviews and from Bell, D. & Ditton, P., *Law: The Old and the New*, Central Australian Aboriginal Legal Aid Service, Canberra, 1980, pp. 16–20.
Comments on men come from personal interviews, statements contained in the Defence Witnesses' Volume III, op. cit., pp. 168–74, and from the dossier cases, collected by Peter Clapin, for the Public Defender's Office.

Page 45, par 1   Bell, D. & Ditton, P., op. cit., p. 93, and from personal interviews with the women from Weipa South.

Page 45, par 2   From Neville Bonner at the seminar prior to Alwyn
                        Peter's trial, organised by the Public Defender's
                        Office, 5 September 1981.

Page 45, par 3   Don Egan's statement taken from the trial
                        transcripts, Day II, p. 150. See also Bell, D., &
                        Ditton, P., op. cit., for discussions on breakdown of
                        traditional kinship structures.

Page 45, par 4   Bell, D., & Ditton, P., op. cit.

Page 45, par 5   Don Egan's statement, taken from the trial trans-
                        cripts, Day II, p. 150.

Page 46, par 2   Excellent accounts of contemporary Aboriginal life
                        can be found in the writings of Charles Perkins and
                        J. Matthews. See Perkins, C., *A Bastard Like Me*,
                        Ure Smith, Sydney, 1975; Matthews, J., *The Two
                        Worlds of Jimmie Barker*, Australian Institute of
                        Aboriginal Studies, Canberra, 1977. The novel by
                        Archie Weller also presents an accurate picture of
                        contemporary Aboriginal life in cities. See Weller,
                        A., *The Day of the Dog*, George Allen & Unwin,
                        Sydney, 1981. Reports of elderly people drinking
                        are increasingly occurring, and come from reserves
                        and communities all over Queensland.

Page 46, par 5   Stanner, W. H., *White Man Got No Dreaming*,
                        ANU Press, Canberra, 1979, p. 47.

Chapter 5: White Man's Drugs

Violence and Alcohol
Page 48, par 2   Figures on the relationship between crime and
                        alcohol come from the statistical analysis of dossier
                        cases collected by Peter Clapin for the Public
                        Defender's Office. The association between crime
                        and alcohol in white society is discussed in
                        Whitlock, F. A., *Drugs: Drinking and Recreational
                        Drug Use in Australia*, Cassell, Sydney, 1980. For a
                        discussion of the socially approved values leading
                        to heavy drinking in Australia see also Sargant, M.,
                        Drinking and Alcoholism in Australia, Longman
                        Cheshire, Melbourne, 1979. It should be recognised
                        that differences between white and black drinking
                        patterns are due, in part at least, to social class
                        differences. Among Europeans, heavy drinking in
                        the working class is often as visible as with
                        Aborigines, and can be seen in public bars, at
                        sporting events and among homeless men on the
                        street. In the white middle class, however, heavy
                        drinking takes place in places such as in private
                        bars, clubs and at home. Without a middle class,
                        Aboriginal drinking as a whole is therefore more
                        visible and open.

Page 48, par 3 ff   Commonwealth Department of Health, *Alcohol in Australia*, Australian Government Publishing Service, Canberra, 1979, pp. 51–62, 113.

Page 49, par 1   These examples were taken from the dossier cases, op. cit., Murder and Manslaughter File, pp. 33 & 376, and Unlawful Wounding File, p. 267.

Page 49, par 2   From Alwyn Peter's Statement Volume II, collected by Peter Clapin for the Public Defender's Office, p. 24.

Page 49, par 3 ff   Duncan's case was taken from the dossier cases, op. cit., Unlawful Wounding File, pp. 334–46, and included a social work report by Anne McKinnon.

Page 50, par 2 ff   Lloyd's case was taken from the dossier cases, op. cit., Unlawful Wounding File, pp. 246–65, and included a social work report by Anne McKinnon.

Page 51, par 1   Quoted from the *Queensland Parliamentary Debates*, 16 September 1981, p. 2101, and taken from *The Medical Journal of Australia*, 2 May 1981.

A Culture of Drinking
Page 51, par 2   The dossiers showed that heavy drinking began among teenagers. The effect that such drinking has on self-esteem and social life has been outlined by Hiram Ryan, among others. I am indebted to Mr Ryan for allowing me to read his report on Aboriginal drinking and for numerous conversations we have had on the topic. His document on Aboriginal drinking has allowed me to conceptualise many of the issues in this area. See Ryan, H., *A New Sub-Culture Within Aboriginal Society: A Collection of Three Papers About Aboriginal Alcohol*, mimeographed report, Brisbane, 1979.

Page 51, par 3   This interview was conducted in the cells of the Brisbane Supreme Court Building, two days before the beginning of the Alwyn Peter trial.

page 51, par 4   From Rachel Peter's statement contained in the Defence Witnesses' Statements Volume III, collected by Peter Clapin for the Public Defender's Office, p. 17. See Kamien, M., 'Aborigines and Alcohol: Intake Effects and Social Implications in a Rural Community in Western New South Wales', *The Medical Journal of Australia*, 1975, 62. The quote from Beckett is cited in Kamien, M., op. cit., p. 296.

Page 52, par 1   From personal interview with Alwyn Peter, op. cit. Taken from the dossier cases, op. cit., Unlawful Wounding File, pp. 356 & 235.

Page 52, par 2   John Cawte at seminar prior to the Alwyn Peter

	trial, organised by the Public Defender's Office, Brisbane, 5 September 1981.
Page 52, par 3	Comparative surveys in this field indicate a recovery rate of 5.5 per cent for Aboriginal alcoholics, compared with 0.4 per cent for Europeans. See Kamien, M., op. cit., p. 296.
Page 53, par 1	It is highly unlikely that Aborigines become drunk after smaller amounts of alcohol consumption than whites. The academic literature is unclear on this point, but personal observation would suggest that Aborigines can hold a given amount of liquor as well, and often better, than whites.
Page 53, par 2	Don Egan's statement taken from the seminar prior to the Alwyn Peter trial, op. cit.
Page 53, par 3	Ibid. Howard Stevens' statement taken from seminar prior to Alwyn Peter trial, op. cit.
Page 53, par 4 ff	Foley's study is reported in an unpublished report, *Concerning Persons Admitted to Aboriginal and Islander Alcohol Relief Program, Cairns*, 1981. The report is available from the Department of Social Work, University of Queensland.
Page 54, par 3 ff	Ibid., pp. 10–14.
Page 55, par 2	From Alwyn Peter's Statement Volume II, collected by Peter Clapin for the Public Defender's Office, p. 36 ff.
Page 55, par 3	Ibid., p. 47 ff.
Page 55, par 4	From statements contained in Defence Witnesses' Statements Volume III, op. cit., pp. 92–93.
Page 55, par 5	Sansom, B., *The Camp at Wallaby Cross*, Australian Institute of Aboriginal Studies, Canberra, 1980, p. 45; Clifford, W., *Aboriginal Criminological Research*, Australian Institute of Criminology, mimeographed workshop report, Canberra, 1981, pp. 12–14; Graves, A., & Collett, A., *A Study of the Nature and Origin of Aboriginal Petty Crime in Port Augusta*, unpublished paper, Adelaide University, 1972.
Page 56, pars 1–2	From statements contained in Defence Witnesses' Statements Volume III, op. cit., p. 101. See also Bell, D., & Ditton, P., *Law: The Old and the New*, Central Australian Aboriginal Legal Aid Service, Canberra, 1980, p. 16; Collman, J., 'Social Order and the Exchange of Liquor: A Theory of Drinking Among Australian Aborigines', *Journal of Anthropological Research*, 1979, 35, pp. 208–24.
Page 56, par 3	House of Representatives Standing Committee

on Aboriginal Affairs, *Alcohol Problems of Aborigines*, Australian Government Publishing Service, Canberra, 1977, p. 17.

Multiple Causes, Multiple Solutions

Page 56, par 4	Ibid., p. 17.
Page 57, par 1	From personal interview with Alwyn Peter, op. cit. From the dossier cases, op. cit., Unlawful Wounding File, p. 239, and Grievous Bodily Harm File, p. 62. Also taken from statements by Maggie Don and Douglas Peter, contained in the Defence Witnesses' Statements Volume III, op. cit., pp. 95 & 102.
Page 57, pars 3–4	An excellent classification of factors associated with alcoholism can be found in Pittman, D. J. (Ed.), *Alcoholism*, Harper & Row, New York, 1967, pp. 3–20.
Page 57, par 5	House of Representatives' Standing Committee on Aboriginal Affairs, op. cit.
Page 57, par 6	Taken from the dossier cases, op. cit., Murder and Manslaughter File, p. 23.
Page 58, par 1	Beckett, J., quoted in Reay, M. (Ed.), *Aborigines Now: New Perspectives in the Study of Aboriginal Communities*, Angus & Robertson, Sydney, 1964, p. 37.
Page 58, par 2	Kamien, M., op. cit., p. 294. From Alwyn Peter's Statement Volume II, op. cit., pp. 11–12.
Page 58, par 3	Harry Eastwell's statement, taken from the trial transcripts, Day IV, p. 216.
Page 58, par 4	Sansom, B., op. cit., p. 49. Taken from personal interviews with residents of the Yarrabah reserve.
Page 59, par 1	House of Representatives Standing Committee on Aboriginal Affairs, op. cit., p. 6. Downing, J., *Cross-Culture Communication with Alcohol*, National Alcohol and Drug Dependence Multidisciplinary Institute, Burgman College, Canberra, mimeographed seminar papers, 1977, p. 7.
Page 59, pars 2–3	Insights into Aboriginal drinking patterns were provided by Ryan, H., op. cit.
Page 59, pars 4 ff	Reynolds, H., 'Aborigines and Settlers: The Australian Experience 1788–1939', *Problems in Australian History*, Cassell, Melbourne, 1972, p. 40. Stanner, W. H., quoted in Reynolds, H., op. cit., p. 43.

Page 60, par 2	Grandfather Koori as quoted in Gilbert, K., *Living Black: Blacks Talk to Kevin Gilbert*, Allen Lane, Ringwood, Victoria, 1977, p. 301.
Page 60, par 3	Ryan, H., op. cit.
Page 60, par 4	Ibid.
Page 60, par 5	Collman, J., op. cit., pp. 212–13.
Page 61, par 1	From the dossier cases, op. cit., Murder and Manslaughter File, pp. 9 & 27.
Page 61, par 2	Collman J., op. cit., pp. 208–09. From the dossier cases, op. cit., Unlawful Wounding File, p. 20.
Page 61, par 3	John Taylor in personal communication with the author.
Page 61, par 4	Noonan, P., *Aboriginal Drinking Behaviour*, unpublished paper, Mackay, 1981, p. 5.
Page 61, par 5	Worrall, J. *European Courts and Tribal Aborigines: A Statistical Collection of Dispositions from the North-West Reserve of South Australia*, unpublished paper presented at 51st ANZAAS Congress, Brisbane, May 1981. Descriptions of glue and petrol sniffing among Aboriginal youths were given to me by officers of the Queensland Department of Children's Services.
Page 62, par 1	Des Frawley's quote was taken from the *Queensland Parliamentary Debates*, State Government Printer, Brisbane, 1981, p. 2101.
Page 62, par 2	Noonan, P., op. cit., p. 3.
Page 62, par 3	Howard Stevens' statement was taken from the seminar organised by the Public Defender's Office, op. cit.
Page 62, par 4	Observations on Douglas House and the Daintree Farm came from my professional and personal involvement with both communities.
Page 63, par 1	These points are discussed in detail in Ward, J., 'Aborigines and Alcohol', in Deihm, A., et. al. (Eds), *Alcohol in Australia: Problems and Programmes*, McGraw-Hill, Sydney, 1978.

Chapter 6: Killing Me Quietly

The Spectre of Imprisonment

Page 64, par 1	Examples are from the dossier cases, Murder and Manslaughter File, pp. 334–46 & 354 ff, collected by Peter Clapin for the Public Defender's Office. See also Armstrong, R., *The Kalkadoons: A Study of an Aboriginal Tribe on the Queensland Frontier*,

William Brooks & Co., Brisbane, 1981; and Roberts,
J. (Ed.), *The Mapoon Story by the Mapoon People*,
International Development Action, Fitzroy,
Victoria, 1975.

Page 64, par 2   Roberts, J. (Ed.), op. cit., pp. 8–13.

Page 64, par 3   See, for example, Wilson, P., & Braithwaite, J.
                        (Eds), *Two Faces of Deviance*, University of
                        Queensland Press, Brisbane, 1978.

Page 64, par 4   See, for example, Eggleston, E., *Fear, Favour or
                        Affection: Aborigines and the Criminal Law in
                        Victoria, South Australia and Western Australia*,
                        ANU Press, Canberra, 1976.

Page 64, par 5 ff   Clifford, W., *Aboriginal Criminological Research*,
                        Australian Institute of Criminology, mimeo-
                        graphed workshop report, Canberra, 1981, p. 28.

Page 65, par 3   Terry White's comments were taken from media
                        statements during October 1981 and confirmed by
                        his Press Secretary, Mr Ted Latta.
                        Quoted from *Senate Hansard*, Australian Govern-
                        ment Publishing Service, 2 April 1981, p. 1125.

Page 65, par 4   Walton, M., *Aborigines and Torres Strait Islanders
                        in Queensland Prisons*, Paper presented to the
                        Criminology Section of the 51st ANZAAS Con-
                        gress, Brisbane, May 1981.

Page 66, par 1   Clapin, P., *A Chronological Account of the Life
                        Story of Alwyn Peter*, unpublished manuscript,
                        Brisbane, 1981, p. 28.

Page 66, par 2   Walton, M., op. cit.; Clapin, P., ibid., p. 29.

Page 66, par 3   See, for example, Brockwell, C. J., *Aborigines and
                        the Law*, Law Department, Australian National
                        University, Canberra, 1979. This is an excellent
                        bibliography dealing with the related material.

Page 67, par 2   See Chapter 2 of this book for details of statistical
                        analyses. Conviction rates reflect police practices
                        and the quality of legal representation, so as a
                        measure of actual crime rates, caution has to be
                        exercised. See also Francis, R., *Migrant Crime in
                        Australia*, University of Queensland Press,
                        Brisbane, 1981; Clifford, W., op. cit., p. 9.

Page 67, par 3   Eggleston, E., op. cit.
                        See also New South Wales Bureau of Crime
                        Statistics and Research, *Statistical Report*, 1976,
                        18.

Page 67, par 4   Eggleston, E., op. cit.
                        From the dossier cases, op. cit.

Page 67, par 5   *Lucas Committee Report of Inquiry into Criminal*

	Law Enforcement in Queensland, State Government Printer, Brisbane, 1977.
Page 68, pars 1–2	Ibid., pp. 78–79.
Page 68, par 3	See *Legal Services Bulletin*, 1978, 3, p. 82.
Page 69, par 3	See Australian Law Reform Commission, *Aboriginal Customary Law–Recognition?*, Discussion Paper 17, Australian Government Publishing Service, Canberra, 1980.
Page 69, par 4	Sackville, R., *Report on Law and Poverty in Australia*, Australian Government Publishing Service, Canberra, 1977.
Page 69, par 5	Eggleston, E., op. cit.
Page 70, par 1	These examples were taken from the dossier cases, op. cit., Murder and Manslaughter File, pp. 157 & 161.
Page 70, par 2	These points have been elaborated in the submission by the Queensland Aboriginal and Islanders Legal Services to the Lucas Committee, op. cit.
Page 70, par 3	Australian Law Reform Commission, op. cit.
Page 70, par 4 ff	Ibid., pp. 18–19.
Page 71, pars 3–4	From the dossier cases, op. cit., Murder and Manslaughter File, pp. 323–35, and from statements contained in Defence Witnesses' Statements Volume III, p. 104, collected by Peter Clapin for the Public Defender's Office.
Page 71, par 5	Taken from John Taylor's *Anthropological Report*, contained in Reports Volume V, p. 61, and collected by Peter Clapin for the Public Defender's Office. Also taken from Maggie Don's statement in the Defence Witnesses' Statements Volume III, op. cit., p. 105.
Page 72, par 1	Taylor, J., op. cit., p. 61.
Page 72, par 2	Australian Law Reform Commission, op. cit., pp. 39–40.

The Other Side of Death
| Page 72, par 3 ff | The data came from Dr J. Jamieson of the Aboriginal Health Programme section of the State Health Department. It contained computer listings of mortality figures by place, age, sex, date and cause of death for all Aborigines from reserves between 1972 and 1980. Only the post-1975 data were used, and were averaged over the five-year period. The causes of death were grouped according to the International Classification of Diseases Index. |

Page 73, pars 2–3   The figures were age and sex standardised to the Queensland population which gives the most accurate comparison possible. The distinction between reserves that received Aborigines from other areas was the same as that used on the violence data, and the further distinction of proximity to white centres was added for these health statistics. Anthropologists Chris Anderson and David Trigger assisted in these calculations.

Page 73, par 4   Sylvia Monk lives on the Gold Coast. She and Dorothy French completed a tour of most Queensland Aboriginal reserves in October 1981. She has kindly made available to me, photographs and transcripts of taped conversations obtained on their tour. This example came from a conversation with Shorty O'Neil in Townsville, 16 October 1981. Her work is not yet published.

Page 73, par 5   *Townsville Daily Bulletin*, 13 November 1979, and *The Australian*, 3 December 1979.

Page 74, pars 1–3   From analysis of Health Department mortality data, op. cit.

Page 74, par 1   *The National Times*, 22 March 1981.

Page 75, par 1   Hollows, F., Royal Australian Council of Opthamologists and the Commonwealth Department of Health, *National Trachoma and Eye Health Programme Report*, Australian Government Publishing Service, Canberra, 1980.

Page 75, par 2   Howard Stevens' statement, taken from the trial transcripts, Day I, p. 27.

Page 75, par 3 ff   *Report on Aboriginal Health in North Queensland by the Wu-Chopperen Medical Service Committee*, unpublished paper, Cairns, 1979.

Page 75, par 4   *Northern Territory News*, 24 September 1980.

Page 76, par 1   Hollows, F., op. cit.

Page 76, par 2   World Council of Churches' Report, *Justice for Aboriginal Australians*, Australian Council of Churches, Sydney, 1981, p. 34.

Page 76, par 3   Clapin, P., op. cit., p. 9 ff.
                       From the statements contained in the Defence Witnesses' Statements Volume III, op. cit., p. 101.
                       From reports collected by Peter Clapin for the Public Defender's Office.

Page 77, par 1   Details of hospital admissions were taken from the Reports Volume V, op. cit., pp. 24–28.

The Consequences
Page 77, par 3 ff   For more detailed discussion of Aboriginal women's

roles see Bell D., & Ditton, P., *Law: The Old and the New*, Central Australian Aboriginal Legal Aid Service, Canberra, 1980.

Page 77, pars 4–5   See Clifford, W., op. cit., pp. 17–24.

Page 78, par 1 ff   Ibid., p. 24 ff.
Taken from the dossier cases, op. cit., Murder and Manslaughter File, p. 149, and from the statements contained in the Defence Witnesses' Statements Volume III, op. cit., p. 174.

Chapter 7: The Official Weapons

On Powerlessness and Prejudice
Page 79, par 1   *The National Times*, 23 August 1981, p. 20.

Page 79, par 2   World Council of Churches Report, *Justice for Aboriginal Australians*, Australian Council of Churches, Sydney, 1981, p. 6.

Page 79, par 3   The World Council of Churches' panel members were described in the Church Journal, *Life and Times*, October 1981, p. 2.

Page 79, par 4   Carl McIntire's credentials are described in *The Courier-Mail*, 26 June 1981, p. 5. Quotes attributed to Carl McIntire came from the paper.

Page 80, pars 1–2   *Department of Aboriginal and Islander Advancement (DAIA) Annual Report*, State Government Printer, Brisbane, 1979 & 1980, introductory pages.

Page 80, par 3   Ibid., introductory pages.

Page 80, par 4   Ken Tomkins' quote was taken from the *Queensland Parliamentary Debates*, State Government Printer, Brisbane, 27 August 1981.

Page 80, par 6   *DAIA Annual Report*, op. cit., 1980, introductory pages.

Page 81, par 2   Smith, B., *The Spectre of Truganini*, Boyer Lectures, Australian Broadcasting Commission, Sydney, 1980, p. 26.

Page 81, par 4   Rowley, C.D., *The Destruction of Aboriginal Society*, ANU Press, Canberra, 1970.

Page 81, par 7 ff   The World Council of Churches' Report, op. cit., p. 17. See also Roberts, J. (Ed.), *The Mapoon Story by the Mapoon People*, International Development Action, Fitzroy, Victoria, 1975.

Page 82, par 1   Clapin, P., *A Chronological Account of the Life Story of Alwyn Peter*, unpublished manuscript, Brisbane, 1981.

Page 82, par 3   Craig, D., 'The Effect of State Policy and Queensland Laws on an Aboriginal Reserve: A Look at

Yarrabah', *Australian Institute of Aboriginal Studies Newsletter*, 1979, 11, pp. 69–71.

Page 83, par 1 ff

Des Pres, T., *The Survivors: An Anatomy of Life in the Death Camps*, Oxford University Press, New York, 1976, p. 99.
Elkins, S., *Slavery*, University of Chicago Press, Chicago, 1959, p. 122.

Page 83, pars 3–4

Des Pres, T., op. cit., and Elkin, S. op. cit.

Page 84, par 1

Armstrong, R., *The Kalkadoons: A Study of an Aboriginal Tribe on the Queensland Frontier*, William Brooks & Co., Brisbane, 1981.

Page 84, pars 2–4

These comments are based on my own observations over a number of years of working within universities and with the media.

Page 84, par 5

Details of this report were published in *Reform*, Australian Law Reform Commission, 1981, 32, p. 83.

Page 85, par 1

Reported in *The National Times*, 23 June 1979, p. 26.

Page 85, par 2

As reported in *The Age*, 12 March 1981 and quoted from comments made in the Senate by Senator Susan Ryan and undisputed by Senator Baume, the Minister for Aboriginal Affairs.

The Political Weapons
Page 85, par 4 ff

Bjelke-Petersen, J., 'Goal is to End Aborigines' Isolation', *South-Burnett Times*, 23 July 1980.

Page 86, par 2

DAIA Annual Report, 1977, op. cit., introductory pages.

Page 86, par 3

Ibid., introductory pages, and *DAIA Annual Report*, 1979, introductory pages.

Page 87, pars 1–2

Nettheim, G., *Victims of the Law: Black Queenslanders Today*, George Allen & Unwin, Sydney, 1981, pp. 60 & 120. See also Doobov, A. & R., 'Queensland: Australia's Deep South', in Stevens, F. (Ed.), *Racism*, II, Australia & New Zealand Book Co., Sydney, 1972, pp. 159–69.

Page 87, par 3

Commissioner for Community Relations Fifth Annual Report, *Queensland Aboriginal Reserves: Policies, Administration and Discrimination*, 1979–80, Appendix K.

Page 87, par 4

Joint Submission of Aborigines and Torres Strait Islanders' Legal Aid Service and the Foundation for Aboriginal and Islander Research Action Concerning Review of Aborigines' and Torres Strait Islanders' Act, II, 1978, pp. 143–47.

Page 88, par 1	Nettheim, G., op. cit., p. 35.

The Economic and Social Weapons

Page 89, par 1	Tomlinson, J., & Davey, S., *Economic and Social Development in Aboriginal Communities in Northern Australia*, unpublished paper, College of Advanced Education, Darwin, 1980, p. 5.
Page 89, pars 3–4	Tomlinson, J., & Davey, S., op. cit., pp. 3–12.
Page 89, par 5	Ibid., p. 5.
Page 90, pars 1–3	Nettheim, G., op. cit., pp. 10 & 56.
Page 90, par 4	Charles Porter's statement quoted from the *Cairns Post*, 5 September 1980.
Page 91, par 1	*The Telegraph*, 14 August 1981.
Page 91, pars 2–3	These points are discussed in detail by Preston, N., 'Black Rights in Queensland', *Semper*, 1 September 1981, p. 15.
Page 91, par 4	The World Council of Churches' Report, op. cit., p. 17.
Page 92, par 1	From a film produced by Comalco Australia, *The Weipa People*, 1979, and available from the National Film Library. It is also relevant to note that neither blacks nor whites can own land or retire at Weipa. Cases exist in which workers for Comalco have tried to buy their company houses when they have retired but were not able to do so. Peter Clapin from the Public Defender's Office also reports that although people cannot own freehold land at Weipa, Woolworths are having a super-market built on land which is freehold. Apparently one rule applies for individuals and another one for organisations.
Page 92, par 3	*DAIA Annual Report*, 1980, op. cit., introductory pages. *North-West Star*, 3 September 1980.
Page 92, par 4	*North-West Star*, 16 October 1979, pp. 5 & 8.
Page 92, par 5	*Townsville Daily Bulletin*, 4 August 1980.
Page 93, pars 1–2	Larsen, K., Dwyer, K., Hartwig, C., Whop, J., & Wyles, V., *Discrimination Against Aborigines and Islanders in North Queensland*, Australian Government Publishing Service, Canberra, 1977, p. 14.
Page 93, pars 3–4	Ibid., p. 19.
Page 94, pars 2–3	Taken from statements contained in Defence Witnesses' Statements Volume III, op. cit., pp. 10–27.

Page 94, par 4   John Taylor's statement is taken from the trial transcripts of *R v Peter*, Day III, p. 234.

Page 94, par 5   Taken from interview with P. Memmott and P. Bycroft, Directors of the Aboriginal Data Archive, published in *The Courier-Mail*, 28 December 1980.

Page 94, par 6   The World Council of Churches' Report, op. cit., p. 9.

Page 95, par 1   Ibid., p. 47.

Page 95, par 2   *North-West Star*, 4 October 1979.

Chapter 8: Ending the Slaughter

A Country's Stigma

Page 96, par 1   See Chapters 4, 5 and 6 for detailed discussions of forced removals, violence and alcohol.
Moodie, P., 'The Health Disadvantages of Aborigines', in Stevens, F. (Ed.), *Racism*, II, Australia and New Zealand Book Co., 1972, p. 240 ff.

Page 96, par 2   Armstrong, R., *The Kalkadoons: A Study of an Aboriginal Tribe on the Queensland Frontier*, William Brooks & Co., Brisbane, 1981.
Roberts, J. (Ed.), *The Mapoon Story by the Mapoon People*, International Development Action, Fitzroy, Victoria, 1975.
Tomlinson, J., & Davey, S., *Economic and Social Development in Aboriginal Communities in Northern Australia*, unpublished paper, College of Advanced Education, Darwin, 1980.

Page 96, par 3   Taken from Coombs, H. C., *Aboriginal Australians 1967–1976*, Murdoch University Press, Perth, 1976, p. 6.

Page 96, par 4   Herbert, X., *Poor Fellow My Country*, Collins, Sydney, 1975, p. 30.

Page 97, par 1   Coombs, H. C., op. cit., pp. 1–16.

Page 98, par 2   From John Taylor's *Anthropological Report*, prepared for the Public Defender's Office, pp. 55–56.

Page 98, pars 3–4   Albrecht, P., 'Talking on Whose Terms?', *The Bulletin*, 8 December 1981, pp. 55 & 56.

Page 100, pars 1–3   Gibb, A., *Report of the Situation of Aborigines on Pastoral Properties in the Northern Territory*, Australian Government Publishing Service, Canberra, 1971.
Paul Everingham's statement taken from *The Age*, 30 October 1981.

Page 100, par 5 ff   Statement by Gale (Convenor of the Campaign Against Racial Exploitation) was taken from *The Australian*, 9 December 1981.

Page 101, par 2	The World Council of Churches' Report, *Justice for Aboriginal Australians*, Australian Council of Churches, Sydney, 1981, p. 6.
Page 101, par 5 ff	Comments taken from the Editorial section of *The Courier-Mail*, 18 November 1981, p. 4.
Page 102, par 2	Joint Submission of Aborigines and Torres Strait Islanders Legal Aid Service and the Foundation for Aboriginal and Islander Research Action Concerning Review of Aborigines and Torres Strait Islanders Act, II, 1978.
New Directions Page 102, par 4	Stanner, W. H., *After the Dreaming*, Boyer Lectures, Australian Broadcasting Commission, Sydney, 1968, p. 57.
Page 102, par 5 ff	Ibid., pp. 45–46.
Page 103, pars 2–3	*The National Times*, 23 August 1981, p. 16.
Page 103, par 4	Rigsby, B., *Aboriginal People, Land Rights and Wilderness in Cape York Peninsula*, Royal Society of Queensland, 1981, 92, pp. 1–10.
Page 103, par 5 ff	Ibid., pp. 1–10.
Page 104, par 3	Woodward, A., *Aboriginal Land Rights Commission, First and Second Reports*, Australian Government Publishing Service, Canberra, 1973 & 1974.
Page 104, par 4	The World Council of Churches' Report, op. cit., p. 15.
Page 105, par 2	Howard Stevens in personal communication with the author, and also taken from Stevens' statements in the trial transcripts, Day I, p. 28.
Page 105, par 3	The World Council of Churches' Report, op. cit., pp. 37–38.
Page 105, par 4	Coombs, H.C., op. cit., p. 8.
Page 106, par 1 ff	Australian Law Reform Commission, *Aboriginal Customary Law — Recognition?*, Discussion Paper 17, Australian Government Publishing Service, Canberra, 1980.
Page 106, par 4 ff	Weisbrot, D., 'Customary Law', *Aboriginal Law Bulletin*, 1981, 1, pp. 3 & 4. Australian Law Reform Commission, op. cit.
Page 107, par 3	Turnbull, M., 'The Law in Black and White', *The Bulletin*, 25 June 1977, p. 18. Weisbrot, D., op. cit., p. 4.
Page 108, par 1	From Joyce Charger's statements at the seminar before the Alwyn Peter trial, organised by the Public Defender's Office, Brisbane, 5 September 1981.

Page 108, par 2   Coombs, H.C., op. cit., p. 9.

Page 108, par 3 ff   Stanner, W. H., op. cit., p. 38 ff.

Page 109, par 2   *The Australian*, 1 October 1981, p. 3.

Page 109, pars 3–4   *The Australian*, 31 December 1981, p. 2.

Page 109, pars 5 ff   An excellent account of the outstation movement can be found in an article by Coombs, H.C., Dexter, B. G., & Hiatt, L. R., 'The Outstation Movement in Aboriginal Australia', *Australian Institute of Aboriginal Studies Newsletter*, 1980, 14, pp. 1–8.

Page 110, par 3   Rowley, C. D., *The Destruction of Aboriginal Society*, ANU Press, Canberra, 1970, p. 12 ff.

Chapter 9: A Choice of Futures

A Chain of Violence
Page 111, par 1 ff   These cases were reported in *The Courier-Mail*, 1 October 1981. Other details were supplied by Peter Clapin from the Public Defender's Office. Details of Russell and his family were supplied by David Trigger, an anthropologist who is involved in researching the history and culture of the people of Doomadgee.

Page 112, pars 2–3   *The Courier-Mail*, 1 October 1981, p. 1.

The Past Repeated
Page 113, par 2 ff   Robertson, G., & Carrick, J., 'The Trials of Nancy Young', *Australian Quarterly*, 1970, 42, pp. 34–46.

Page 113, par 4 ff   Ibid., pp. 35–36.

Page 115, par 2 ff   Mr Justice Dunn's statements are taken from the trial transcripts, Day V, pp. 1–3.

Page 115, par 6 ff   See Najman, J., 'Victims of Homicide: An Epidemiologic Approach to Social Policy', *The Australian and New Zealand Journal of Criminology*, 1980, 13, pp. 272–80.

Page 116, par 1   Ibid., p. 279.

A Man Called Alwyn Peter
Page 116, par 5   Ivor Jones' statement was taken from the trial transcripts, Day IV, p. 257.

Page 116, par 6 ff   Matt Foley's statements were taken from the trial transcripts, Day IV, p. 177.

Page 117, par 4 ff   During the last week of January 1982, the Queensland media began asking why Alwyn Peter had not been released from prison. In response, the Minister for Welfare Services, Terry White, announced that Alwyn would be released during the first week of February. Defending the Parole

Board's decision not to give reasons to prisoners for delayed parole or rejections of parole application, White said that it could harm a prisoner to be told that his psychological condition precluded his release (*The Courier-Mail*, 26 January 1982, p. 1). In the year to 30 June 1980, 188 people were released on parole from 661 applicants. Of the 126 people whose release, as with Alwyn's, was recommended by the sentencing court, only 77 were released. Psychological condition would provide grounds for refusing parole to only a handful of the people the Board declined to release. One can only speculate as to the harm that would be done to the psychological condition of prisoners by not telling them the reasons for delayed or refused parole. In defending the four months it took to release Alwyn from prison, despite Mr Justice Dunn's recommendation for immediate parole, Terry White argued that a detailed program had to be worked out for Alwyn's rehabilitation after release. Four months seems an inordinately long time to work out such a program, particularly if done without consultation with the parolee and his family. (Mike Kennedy of the Prisoners' Action Group supplied the above figures).

Page 118, par 5

Although the use of psychiatry in 'changing' Aboriginal behaviour has not yet been fully researched, there is evidence that psychiatrists often apply Western-style therapy to Aborigines without any consideration of the cultural and historical problems associated with a repressed minority group. See *Aborigines and Mental Health: Hitting Our Heads Against a Brick Wall*, Australian National Association for Mental Health, Sydney, 1981.

Index

Aboriginal and Islander Alcohol Relief Programme, iv, 53
Aboriginal and Islander Medical Service, 74
Aboriginal and Torres Strait Islander Legal Services, 3, 87-8, 102
Aboriginal Development Commission, 91, 103
Aboriginal, activists, 80, 86; affairs, 84-6, 106, 109, 116, 118; children, 36, 108; control, 62, 107; culture, 38, 46-7, 69, 84, 108; customs, 69; existence, 35, 84; groups, 37, 43, 45, 51, 59, 91, 98, 104, 105; issues, 103; matters, viii, 69, 79, 103; owners, 104; problems, 69, 72, 80, 96-7, 102; sacred sites, 90, 91, 98; social life, 45, 51, 56, 58, 62, 67, 71, 84, 93; women, 15, 44-5, 48; workers, 87, 89, 112; workforce, 85
Aboriginality, ix, 9, 43, 46
Aboriginal reserves and communities, viii, 1-5, 9-20, 27-9, 32, 70, 79, 100; alcohol on 48, 50, 53, 61; cohesion in 18-9, 108; conditions on 20, 73-6, 87, 94-115; control of 76-109; councils on 44-5, 62, 81; dwellers on 9-16, 61-71, 81, 83, 100, 102, 116; formation of 78; fragmentation of 77, 111; mining on 1, 82, 91; violence on 3-18, 48, 71, 106-18
Aborigines, part- 86; Queensland 68, 84-7, 102, 111, 115; urban 9, 43, 67, 86, 108
Act(s), Aboriginal Relics Preservation 91; Aborigines and Torres Strait Islander 9; Local Government Aboriginal Lands, 81, 90
adolescence, 2, 14, 16, 58, 61, 77
aggression, 7-11, 22, 31, 33, 40-51, 64, 66
Albrecht, P., 98
alcohol, 16, 20, 37, 44-61, 80, 96, 112; and violence, 17, 22, 45, 48, 63, 71, 72, 115; availability of 17-19, 50, 57; beer, wine, spirits, 2, 11, 16, 22, 25, 49, 52-60; clinics, 62; consumption, 48-55, 61-2, 74; culture, 57-62; hotstuff, 2, 49; poisoning, 74; rehabilitation, 115, 117; see also drinking.

alcoholism, ix, 1, 48, 56-7, 69, 76, 97
Amax Petrol, 89
Anderson, C., viii,
anger, 13, 23, 26, 29, 32, 71
anthropologist(s), viii, 17, 28-34, 61, 71, 91-115
argument(s), 13, 15, 23, 34, 49, 69, 93-4
Armstrong, R., 84
arrest(s), 55, 67, 70
assault(s), 2-5, 9-16, 48, 66-7, 71; aggravated 67; serious 48, 66-7, 116; sexual 45
assimilation, 83, 85, 89, 97-8, 100, 102
Association of Professional Anthropologists and Archaeologists, 91
Aurukun, 18, 20, 49, 62, 81-91, 111-12
Australian Bureau of Statistics, 65
Australian Institute of Criminology, viii, 55, 64
Australian Law Reform Commission, 69-70, 72, 106

bail, 14, 67, 70, 113
beating(s), 5, 14; by parents, 40-1, 45, 111
Beckett, J., 51, 58,
behaviour, patterns of 46; disorderly 67
Bell, D., & Ditton, P., 34, 44
Bjelke-Petersen, J., 79, 85-7, 100-3
bloodletting, 30
Bonner, N. 74
Brennan, F., viii
Brisbane, 1, 8, 19, 43, 74, 81, 113, 117
brutality, 68, 102
Bouganville, 89

Camooweal, 92
camp(s), 81, 83, 92
canteen(s), 6, 11-19, 23, 27, 52-3, 62
Cape York Peninsula, 103-4
cases of, Duncan, 49-51, 64; George, 14; Geraldine, 5, 14, 66; Harold, 14, 19, 60, 84; John 19; Oscar, 6-7, 10, 60, 64, 118; Percy, 11-19, 26; Russell, 16-7, 111-13, 118
Cawte, J., 52
ceremonies, 17, 30, 31, 44, 58, 94, 104

charge(s), 67-8, 113
Cherbourg, 72
childhood, 18, 40, 76
children, 58, 65, 76, 111-14, 118; love of 45
christians, 11, 79-80, 110
church(es), 38, 79, 80, 90
clan(s), 36-7, 45, 56, 100
Clapin, P., vii-viii, 29, 113
Clifford, W., 64-5
Colless, R., 53-4
Collman, J., 60
Comalco, 38-40, 89-92
Commonwealth Games, 1
community(ies), 78, 83, 88, 101; contemporary, 34, 72; disintegration, 16, 21;
   fringe, 59-60; leaders, 43-4, 112; life, 36-7,
   46, 48, 62; Queensland, 86, 104;
   therapeutic, 62; white, 93
conditions, 1, 21, 59, 61, 92-6, 100-16
convictions, 13, 65-7, 78, 114, 117
Cook, Captain James, 35-6
Coombs, H., 97, 105, 108
council(s), 37, 62, 81-90, 109-18; city, 92
Courier-Mail, viii
court(s), 1-3, 42, 45, 67-87, 90, 106-15;
   appearances, 18, 49, 69, 80, 108
Craig, D., 82
criminal, activity, 14, 101-2; charges, 7, 13-4,
   55, 67-8; justice system, 66-8, 77, 106-8
crime(s), viii, 45, 69-77, 84, 107-14; and
   alcohol, 48, 55; and imprisonment, 67;
   figures, 67; on reserves, 14, 56, 107; rates,
   18, 67, 116; violent, 3, 44, 71, 112
cultural, conflict, 69-70; factors in violence,
   17, 37; patterns, 72; position, 67
culture, 27, 38, 45; Aboriginal, 69-70, 76,
   83-4, 108; alcohol, 57-62; conflict, 61, 69;
   drinking, 48, 51; European, 46, 82;
   traditional, 18
Cunnamulla, 113-15, 118

death(s), ix, 2-6, 10-16, 20, 28, 30, 32, 44, 51,
   59, 64-74, 77, 96, 105, 112, 115-19
delinquent(s), 65
denigration, 80, 83
DePres, T., 83-4
deprivation, 2, 20, 116
destruction, 7, 39, 112, 118; of culture, 84
disease(s), 8, 50, 73, 75-6, 105, 114; see also
   health, illnesses
displacement of Aborigines, 18-9, 21, 76, 113
disputes, 15, 37, 61
Don, F., 37, 40
Don, M., 24, 40-3, 57, 71, 76, 92, 114
Doomadgee, 18, 30, 62, 69, 111, 112
dossier(s), 3, 4, 11, 34, 45, 49, 61, 70-1
Douglas House, ix, 54, 62
Downing, J., 59
Dreamtime, 34, 36, 37, 46

drinking, 6, 14, 16, 62, 69, 94, 117-18; and
   crime, 55; behaviour, 53, 56-7, 61; causes
   of 62; groups, 11, 61; habits, 48, 49, 60; in
   hotels, 54, 93, 94; on reserves, 50, 53, 56-7;
   parties, 49; patterns, 48, 53, 54, 59, 60, 62;
   problems, 50, 52, 54, 115; reasons for 57,
   112; sessions, 50-2, 57
drug(s), 20, 46, 48, 51, 61, 74, 77
drunken brawls, 12, 14, 28, 72, 101
Dunn, Mr Justice, 1-2, 42, 75, 111, 115, 117
Dunstan, D., 89

Eastwell, H., 33, 58
economic, 20; inequality, 116; resources, 89
Edward River, 18, 61
education, 9, 20, 59, 63, 95, 102, 103, 118
Egan, D., 46, 53
Eggleston, E., 67
Elkin, S., 83-4
employment, 9, 19, 21, 44, 59, 89, 93, 95, 98;
   see also unemployment
environmental factors, 76
evidence, vii, 2, 3, 58, 62, 69, 73, 110-15
exploitation, 7-9, 60, 90, 96, 108

family/families, 10, 20, 25, 39, 43, 75, 76, 78,
   92; extended, 46, 112; life, 44-5; members,
   22, 54, 65, 66, 111, 112; patterns, 43-4;
   structures, 43, 77, 94; support, 117;
   violence within, 45, 56, 112
fight(s), 2, 11, 13-15, 20-8, 31, 34, 46, 49-58,
   62, 72, 78
fishing, 1, 41, 57, 110
Foley, M., 27, 28, 42, 53-4, 116-17
food, 36, 60, 61, 78, 110-11, 113; gathering, 1,
   37, 44; preparation, 17, 36, 44
Four Corners, 115
freehold title, 101, 104-5
frustration(s), 11, 33, 45, 74, 86

Gilbert, D., 1-3, 16, 22-4, 33, 49, 71, 96,
   115-19
Gilbert, K., 9-46
girlfriend(s), vii, 13, 44, 49, 96, 111-15
Goodin, J., 29
government(s), 18, 38, 63, 76, 84, 90, 96, 98,
   118
government, federal, 75, 80-90, 95, 98, 101-9;
   Department of Aboriginal Affairs, 89, 109;
   Department of Health, 48; policies, 97-8
government, Queensland, viii, 38-9, 62-5,
   75-8, 83-6, 90-105; Department of Aboriginal and Islander Advancement, 28, 44,
   66, 75, 80-7, 92; Department of Native
   Affairs, 40; officials, ix, 64, 69, 81-8, 94,
   102; policies, 65, 78, 80-6, 92, 95, 104, 110
guilt, 71, 96, 119

health, 9, 20-1, 28, 63, 65, 84, 102, 118;

Aboriginal, 64, 75, 76; and alcohol, 51, 59; problems of 74, 105; services, 76, 105; *see also* disease, illnesses, injuries,
Herbert, X., 97
historical factors, vii, 7, 59, 91
history, 38, 97, 102, 108; of Kalkadoons, 84; medical, 76
Hollows, F., 75, 76
home(s), 1, 11, 19, 22, 38, 82, 92, 117; Aboriginal, 94; burnt by police, 40, 64; spiritual, 103, 104; traditional, 40
homelands of Aborigines, 8, 18, 97, 110
homelessness, 69, 75, 92-93, 103-105, 107, 110
homicide(s), 2, 4, 12-16, 115-16; and alcohol, 48; offenders of 18; rates, 4, 67
hopelessness, 9
Hopevale, 50, 72
hospital, 114; admissions, 76-77; records, 81.
house(s), 12-24, 39, 75, 82-3, 87, 93-5, 114 burning down of 81
housing, 9, 59, 63, 76, 78, 92-5, 102-3, 106, 118
hunting, 19, 39, 57, 96, 110

illness(es), 2, 20, 44, 73, 75, 77
imprisonment, 43-4, 64, 66-7, 72, 77-8, 101
income, 20, 44, 60, 70, 101, 110
infection(s), 76-7
initiation(s), 31, 58
injury, injuries, 12, 13, 22, 28, 30-36, 58, 64, 71; *see also* health, unlawful wounding
integration, 81, 83, 89, 92, 104
International Council of Churches, 79
intoxicated, 111
institutions for juveniles, 77
isolation of reserves, 17

jails, *see* prisons
Jardine, F., 37-8
jealousy, 10, 16-7, 20, 24, 56, 71, 111
Jimmy, J., 37-8, 40, 42
Jones, I., 28, 32-3, 116
judge(s), 21, 69, 115
jury, 69, 113
justice, 72, 90, 114
Justice(s) of the Peace, 69, 83
justice system; *see* criminal justice system
juvenile(s), 65-6, 78,

Kamien, M., 51
Kennedy, L., 37-8,
killing(s), vii, ix, 2-5, 10-16, 20-8, 31, 37, 49, 50, 68, 71, 96, 111, 118
Killoran, P., 39, 86
kinship, 36, 43, 56, 59, 84

Labor party, 84

land, 8-9, 36-8, 42, 86, 89, 98, 101-3, 110, 118-19; control of 77, 101; crown 104; displacement from 45, 64; dispossession of 60; expropriation, 7, 97; freehold 79; loss of 9, 44, 92, 104; love of 46, 117-18; owners of 109; removal from 40; reserve 39, 91, 104-5; rights, 70, 86, 98, 100-5; sacredness of 91; securing 89; title to 102; traditional 76, 92, 96, 103, 109
Langton, M., 43
language, 1, 9, 17, 38, 86, 96, 108, 110; obscene 66-7
Lanley, L., 112
Larsen, K., 93
law(s), 7, 69, 81-6, 91, 109, 112, 114; by- 9, 82-3; criminal, 68, 106; traditional, 60, 70-2, 98, 106-7, 110; white, 69, 87, 107, 110
lawyers, 69, 107
leases, 39, 90-1, 101, 104; pastoral, 100
legislation, 87, 89-90, 100-1
Liberal party, 97
lifestyle, 43
Lincoln, R., 72, 117-18
Lockhart, 18
lock-up, 23, 66

Mace, M., ix
magistrate(s), 69, 85
malnutrition, 76
management, 87, 90, 104
manslaughter, 1, 4-5, 68, 113-16
    see also homicide, murder,
marriage, 5, 44, 78, 106
Maoris, 8
Mapoon, 18-19, 27, 38-41, 57, 64, 89, 92, 117-18; destruction, 40, 96; people of, 8, 14, 20, 36-40, 81, 96
Mapoon Story, the 38-9, 42, 82
McElwain, D., viii,
McKinnon, A., 25, 27
McMahon, W., 97
media, 84, 96, 113-14
mineral(s), 86, 90, 96, 101
mining, 1, 89-91, 98, 103, 105; companies, 1, 39, 82, 89-90
mission(s), 2, 6, 18, 38-9, 109-11
missionaries, 37-8, 58
Monk, S., viii, 73
morbidity rates, *see* statistics
Moreton Bay Courier, 7
Mornington Island, 16, 81, 88, 90-1, 95, 111-12
mortality rates, *see* statistics, rates
Mount Isa, 69, 92
mourning, 30, 112
multinational(s), 89, 91, 102
Mukherjee, S., viii,
murder, 1-5, 9-11, 17, 38, 68, 97, 101, 115-16; mass, 83; *see also* homicide, manslaughter

Nabalco, 89
National party, 101-2
National Times, 103
National Trachoma and Eye Health-
   Program, 75-6
native(s), 36
New Guinea, 107
New South Wales, 84-5, 91, 105; Bureau of
   Crime Research and Statistics, 67
Noonan, P., ix, 61
Noonkanbah, 89-90
Northern Territory, 55, 59, 74, 89, 91,
   100-9

O'Connor, B., vii, 3, 70, 112
offence(s), 10, 55, 67, 70-1, 108; minor, 56,
   64, 67, 107; serious, 71; stealing, 66;
   violent, viii, 3, 6-7, 116
offender(s), 4, 11, 14, 19-20, 67, 72;
   Aboriginal, 10; and drinking, 48-9, 52, 57;
   characteristica of 14, 48, 66, 71; juvenile,
   58; minor, 69; violent viii, 10, 13, 51, 108
O'Neill, S., 42-3, 80
oppression, ix, 29
outstation movement, 62, 109-10

Palm Island, 18-19, 38, 42, 52, 72-3
parole, 113-5, 117
past, 7, 9, 45-6, 58, 86, 95-7, 107, 113
pastoralist(s) 7, 38, 64; *see also* settlers
paternalism, 63, 83, 102-9, 119
'payback' 72
Peter, Alwyn, vii, ix, 1-7, 22, 71, 82, 92, 96,
   111, 115; ancestors of vii, 36, 92, 117; and
   drinking, 2-3, 22, 24, 49, 51, 55, 57-8, 71;
   and Mapoon, 19, 40-2, 117, 118; and
   prison, 66, 117; and self-mutilation, 23-9,
   33; and violence, 14, 64, 71, 94; case of viii,
   2-4, 110; childhood of 14, 40, 45; defence of,
   vii, 112; future of, 115-17; health of 77;
   history of vii, ix, 29, 119; life of vii, 3, 29,
   60, 84, 119; mobility of 19; relatives of 2,
   18, 20, 42-4, 55, 82; trial of 16, 26, 108,
   113-14; tribe of 36
Peter Amy, 25-7, 34
Peter, Douglas, 57
Peter family, 1, 5, 14, 25, 40, 42, 76, 78
Peter, Rachel, 14, 23-4, 39-43, 51, 76-7, 92,
   114
Peter Raymond, 25
Peter Sidney, 5, 14, 25, 55, 66, 92
Peter, Simon, 22-3, 37, 40, 77
Peterson, D., viii
percentages, *see* rates, statistics
pneumonia, 77, 114
poisoning, 7, 64, 89
police, 2-9, 12, 18, 22, 39, 40, 60, 69, 85, 102;
   action, 71; Aboriginal or native 5, 69, 81-4,
   87, 106, 116; community 51; Edward
River, 11; escort, 89; harrassed by 68, 92-3;
   insensitivity, 70; inspector, 68; interrogation, 70, 77; Queensland, 109; records of
   interview, 12; watch houses, 55; white, 5,
   39, 116
politicians, 1, 21, 74, 79, 81, 112
polygyny, 44
population(s), 17-18, 65, 72; Aboriginal, 8-9,
   65, 101-2, 107, 109; Australian, 4, 51, 65,
   113; on reserves, 4
power(s), 44-5, 79, 81-3, 87-8, 95, 106; legal,
   91, 98, 100-1; political, 101
powerlessness, 9, 56, 79, 81-5, 101-16
poverty, 43, 103, 114
prejudice,
   see racial prejudice
prison(s), 2, 5, 63, 65, 77-8, 96, 108, 113,
   117-18; figures on, 65; maximum security,
   10, 33; sentences, 19, 116; *see also*
   imprisonment
progress, ix, 92, 96, 106
prohibition of alcohol, 57, 60, 62
psychiatrist(s), viii, 28, 33, 52, 58, 115-18
psychologist(s), viii, 33, 93
punishment(s), 10, 16, 32, 37, 42, 60, 72, 108,
   116; traditional, 15, 71
purposelessness, 84

Queensland, 42, 55, 62-85, 91, 101-9, 113,
   118
Queenslanders, 1
Queenslander, The 10

race, 1, 8, 85
racial, discrimination, 68, 93-5; identity, 97;
   prejudice, 79, 93; pride, 108
racism, 65, 68-9, 93, 95, 108, 113-4
rape, 44, 45
rates, homicide, 115-16; crime, 67, 69;
   imprisonment, 64, 69, 77; morbidity,
   105-6, 113; mortality, 72, 75, 77, 105-6,
   113; recovery 53; serious assault, 116
Reid, R., 39
relationship(s), 16, 36, 51
de facto, 5, 19, 44; family, 44, 78; of offender
   to victims, 10, 49, 56; traditional, 45, 59;
   within groups, 60
relative(s), 7, 10, 20-9, 40-3, 50, 57, 87,
   110-14; and drinking, 54-5; killing of a 111;
   of Deidre, 117
reserve(s), 16-18, 78, 81-2, 104, 108;
   Aboriginal, 16-18, 97, 101, 106, 114, 116;
   councillors, 79; life on 15, 46; mining on,
   89-91; origins of, 17; Queensland, 16, 43-5,
   58, 67, 71-2, 82-8, 115; social conditions on,
   95, 107; staff on, 87
right(s) 39, 86-98, 100-3; mining, 90
ritual(s), 1, 9, 30-1, 61, 84
Rosser, B., 27
Rowley, C., 81

sanitation, 76, 105-6, 114
Sansom, B.,
scars, 23, 27-8, 33
self-control, 46, 51, 71, 102, 110
self-destruction, 25, 31, 51, 97
self-destructive acts, 27, 29, 33, 55, 101
self-determination, 46, 85, 97-8, 102
self-esteem, 9, 51, 56-61, 108-9, 111, 116
self-help movement, 53
self-mutilation, 1, 22-9, 31, 33-4, 77, 84, 97, 112; and alcohol, 48; females and 34
sentence(s), 5, 65, 67, 69, 85, 108, 113-15, 117
settlement(s), 79, 93, 101; European, 95, 115; forced, 92, 111; Mapoon, 39, 40
settlers, white, 7, 37-8, 48, 112
sewerage, 73, 106
sexual 'depravity', 7; exploitation, 62; favours, 48; intercourse, 13, 16
shire(s), 81, 90, 95
slaves, American, 83
Smith, B., 81
social,
    action, 96; change, 46, 77; conditions on reserves, 7, 9, 20; context, 15; control, 37, 56, 106-7; factors in violence, 17, 113; forces, 116; life on reserves, 93; myths, 92; networks, 103; organisations, 98, 106; patterns, 61; planning, 86; problems, 57, 69, 81; security, 43; situations, 57; workers, 11-15, 25, 42, 52-3, 65, 118
societies, 10, 18, 85; Aboriginal, 7, 9, 43, 45, 48, 56, 98, 112; Australian, 10, 95, 97; destruction of 21; traditional, 19, 30, 37, 44-5, 71; white, 9, 10, 11, 46, 60, 83
sociologist(s), 72, 115
South Africa, 100-1
South Australia, 56, 89, 91, 109
spearing, 32, 37, 71, 108
spirituality, 42
Stanner, W., 32-3, 60
statistics, 7, 12-13, 80, 101; alcohol, 48, 51, 53, 54, 56; crime rates, 5, 67; employment, 95; imprisonment, 64, 65; mortality 72-3, 75, 106; violence, 14
Stevens, H., 28, 53, 62, 75, 105
stress, 31-2, 59, 61, 74, 110
Sturgess, D., vii-viii, 2, 113
suicide(s), 28-9, 33
Sykes, B., ix
syphilis, 74

Taylor, J., viii, 28, 61, 71-2, 94
territorial violations, 37
Tipperary, 85
Toeboy, H., 37
Tomlinson, J., & Davey S., 89
Torres Strait Islander(s), ix, 14, 20, 95
Townsville, 19, 42, 66, 73-4, 80, 92-3, 113
trachoma, 75
traditional, 18, 31-2, 34, 40, 101; authority, 77; communication, 100; communities, 15,
43, 56; culture, 17, 30, 95; food, 42; lifestyles, 97; owners, 90; people, 33; practices, 32; society, 10, 30, 32-3, 44, 56; ways, 9, 16, 19, 21, 43, 58, 60, 62, 71, 83
treaties, 8, 109
trial(s), vii, viii, 16, 26, 42, 69, 101, 112-17
tribal, Aborigines, 73; disharmony, 18-19; ground, 40; land, 18; law, 15
tribe(s), 1, 8, 10, 17-20, 30-6, 43, 60, 72; Arunta, 30; Bwgcolmans, 42; Central Australian, 31; Kalkadoons, 7-8, 31, 38, 64, 84; Mapoon, 37; Pitjantjantjara, 89; River Darling, 30;
Tjungundji, 36; Vasse River, 30; Warburton Range, 32; Warramunga, 31; Wiimbaio, 31; Yupungatti, 36
Trigger, D., 30

unemployment, 2, 43, 59, 69, 76, 90, 95; benefits, 82
unlawful wounding, 4, 14, 19, 49
Universal Declaration of Human Rights, 87
University, James Cook, viii, 29
University of Queensland, viii, ix
Urandangie, 92
uranium, 89, 91
United States, 62, 107; Indians, 5, 8

victim(s), 7, 10, 19, 72, 96; and alcohol, 48; of violence, 12-14, 45, 68, 116
violence, viii, ix, 2-13, 22-7, 31-7, 69-73, 77, 84, 94, 96, 111-18
    among youth, 61; and abuse, 44, 45; and alcohol, 45, 48, 50, 61, 115; and women, 10, 46; cases of, 10, 112; causes of, 17, 20, 116; climate of, 14; community, 16, 58, 63; criminal 48; patterns of 16; rates, 13, 17, 18; stabbings, 1, 2, 10, 49; towards others, 32, 51; within families, 58
wages, 45, 87, 114
Wakefield, T., 2, 75, 120
Walton, M., 65-6
water, 36, 73-6, 92, 106, 113
weapons, 2, 5-6, 9-15, 22-3, 27, 40, 49-50, 70-1, 79, 84; economic, 89; political, 85; social, 89
Weipa, 2, 18-20, 27, 39, 40, 42, 55, 89
Weipa South, 1-7, 14, 19-29, 42, 45, 52-3, 57, 66, 71-2, 82, 92, 100, 108, 113-18
Weisbrot, D., 106
welfare worker(s), 28-9, 62
Welley, A., 30-46
Western Australia, 30, 85, 89
whites, 9, 17, 34, 46, 53, 64, 67, 73-9, 81-2, 91-8, 101, 106
Williams, Mr Justice, 112
World Council of Churches, 38, 76, 79, 80, 91, 95
Wymara, E., 27, 43

Yarrabah, 18, 29, 59, 72, 82, 87, 100, 109
Young, Nancy, 113-118